Ober • Johnson • Zimmerly

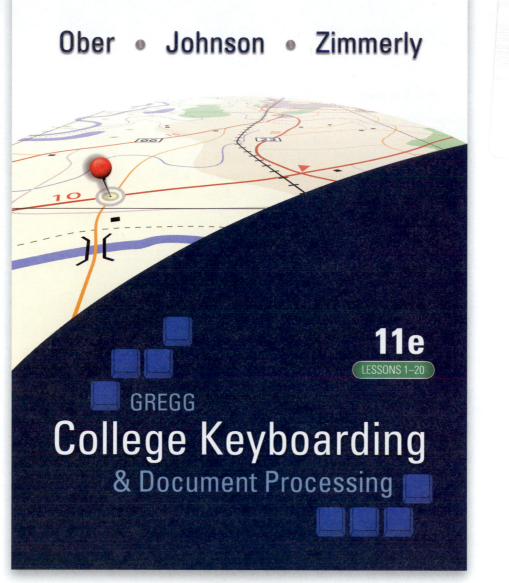

11e
LESSONS 1–20

GREGG
College Keyboarding
& Document Processing

Scot Ober
Ball State University
Jack E. Johnson
University of West Georgia
Arlene Zimmerly
Los Angeles City College

Visit the *College Keyboarding* Web site at **www.mhhe.com/gdp11**

Connect
Learn
Succeed™

GREGG COLLEGE KEYBOARDING & DOCUMENT PROCESSING, LESSONS 1–20

Published by McGraw-Hill, a business unit of The McGraw-Hill Companies, Inc., 1221 Avenue of the Americas, New York, NY, 10020. Copyright © 2011 by The McGraw-Hill Companies, Inc. All rights reserved. Previous editions © 1957, 1964, 1970, 1979, 1984, 1989, 1994, 1997, 2002, 2006, and 2008. No part of this publication may be reproduced or distributed in any form or by any means, or stored in a database or retrieval system, without the prior written consent of The McGraw-Hill Companies, Inc., including, but not limited to, in any network or other electronic storage or transmission, or broadcast for distance learning.

Some ancillaries, including electronic and print components, may not be available to customers outside the United States.

This book is printed on acid-free paper.

9 10 11 12 13 RMN/RMN 1 0 9 8 7 6 5 4

ISBN 978-0-07-734422-1
MHID 0-07-734422-7

Vice President/Editor in Chief: *Elizabeth Haefele*
Vice President/Director of Marketing: *John E. Biernat*
Executive editor: *Scott Davidson*
Director of Development, Business Careers: *Sarah Wood*
Editorial coordinator: *Alan Palmer*
Marketing manager: *Tiffany Wendt*
Lead digital product manager: *Damian Moshak*
Senior digital product manager: *Lynn M. Bluhm*
Digital product specialist: *Randall Bates*
Director, Editing/Design/Production: *Jess Ann Kosic*
Project manager: *Marlena Pechan*
Senior production supervisor: *Janean A. Utley*
Senior designer: *Marianna Kinigakis*
Senior photo research coordinator: *Lori Kramer*
Digital production coordinator: *Brent Dela Cruz*
Digital developmental editor: *Kevin White*
Outside development house: *Debra Matteson*
Cover credit: *© Robert Adrian Hillman/Shutterstock*
Cover design: *Jessica M. Lazar*
Interior design: *Jessica M. Lazar and Laurie J. Entringer, BrainWorx Studio, Inc.*
Typeface: *11/13.5 Adobe Garamond Pro*
Compositor: *Lachina Publishing Services*
Printer: RR Donnelley, Menesha
Credits: The credits section for this book begins on page I-6 and is considered an extension of the copyright page.

The Library of Congress has cataloged the single volume edition of this work as follows

Ober, Scot, 1946–
      Gregg college keyboarding & document processing. Lessons 1–120 / Scot Ober,
Jack E. Johnson, Arlene Zimmerly. — 11th ed.
        p. cm
      Includeds index.
      ISBN-13: 978-0-07-337219-8 (Lessons 1–120)
      ISBN-10: 0-07-337219-6 (Lessons 1–120)
      ISBN-13: 978-0-07-734422-1 (Lessons 1–20)
      ISBN-10: 0-07-734422-7 (Lessons 1–20)
      ISBN-13: 978-0-07-731936-6 (Lessons 1–60)
      ISBN-10: 0-07-731936-2 (Lessons 1–60)
      ISBN-13: 978-0-07-731940-3 (Lessons 61–120)
      ISBN-10: 0-07-731940-0 (Lessons 61–120)
      1. Word processing—Problems, exercises, etc. 2. Keyboarding—Problems, exercises,
etc. 3. Commercial correspondence—Problems, exercises, etc. 4. Report writing—Problems,
exercises, etc. I. Johnson, Jack E. II. Zimmerly, Arlene. III. Title. IV. Title: Gregg college
keyboarding and document processing.

Z52.3.G74 2011
652.3'0076—dc22   2009037843

The Internet addresses listed in the text were accurate at the time of publication. The inclusion of a Web site does not indicate an endorsement by the authors or McGraw-Hill, and McGraw-Hill does not guarantee the accuracy of the information presented at these sites.

www.mhhe.com

Welcome to
Gregg College Keyboarding & Document Processing
11th Edition

Your complete learning/teaching *system*
Your guide to success

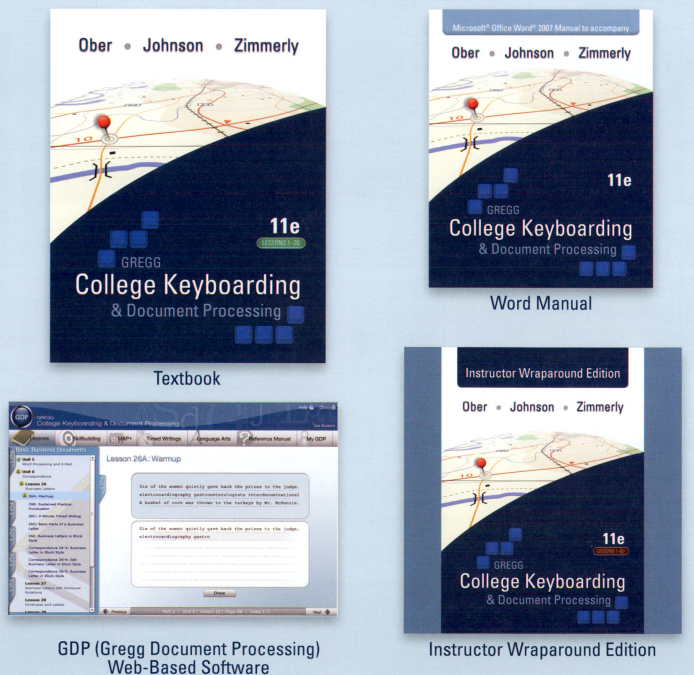

Textbook

Word Manual

GDP (Gregg Document Processing)
Web-Based Software

Instructor Wraparound Edition

Online GDP Software
New! Online functionality
Same program; *now* Web-based

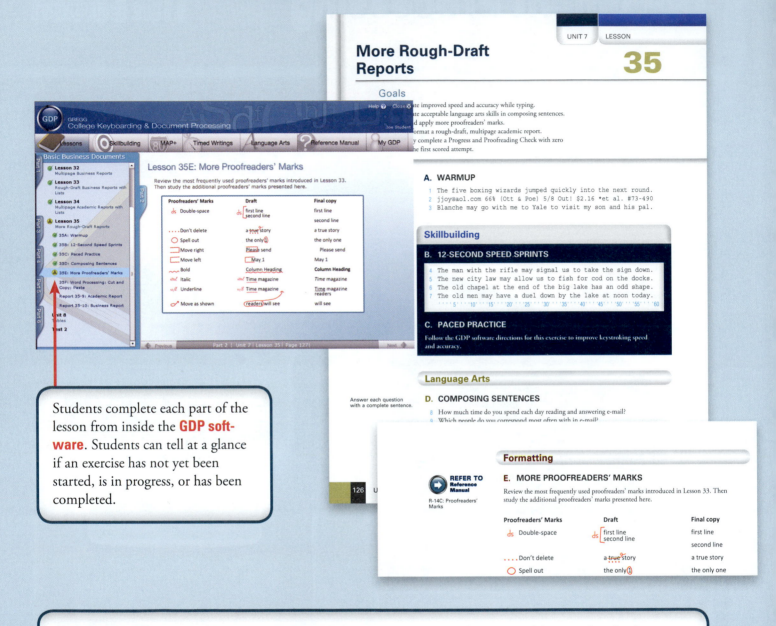

Students complete each part of the lesson from inside the **GDP software**. Students can tell at a glance if an exercise has not yet been started, is in progress, or has been completed.

This online software now offers greater accessibility for use at home, in class, and in labs—perfect for distance learning! Its easy-to-use interface makes this system simple for both you and your students . . . so that you spend more time teaching the skills you want, not learning the program. The GDP software also now allows for automatic keystroking and format scoring.

With GDP's new online functionality, updates are now seamless.

MAP+
The best just got better!

MAP+ **(Misstroke Analysis and Prescription)** is a *diagnostic tool* within GDP/11 that analyzes each student's pretest misstrokes and prescribes individualized remediation drills based on a powerful new scoring algorithm. MAP+ includes these features:

- **New! Unlimited drill lines**—*Now begin with Lesson 1.*

- **Interactive**—Features a streamlined interactive screen, which allows students to click anywhere for intensive practice on that key or kind of reach.

- **Continuous new drills**—Generate three *new* drill lines every time the student clicks a key or specific reach.

- **New! Deeper content**—Allows students to take a pretest and practice either alphabetic copy, numbers, or numbers and symbols.

- **Integrated**—Is a required part of each unit, although students can access MAP+ at any time from the lesson menu.

New! Enrichment Pages
More drill lines for faster touch-typing skills

Enrichment pages appear at the end of each of the new-key lessons (Lessons 1–20). If you want your students to have additional practice on each of these lessons, you can assign them as desired.

Using the GDP system, you can customize GDP to include Enrichment pages as part of the lesson requirements.

With **MAP+**, students also have unlimited new practice drills—*beginning with Lesson 1*. Every time they access MAP+ for a specific lesson, new drill lines appear that contain only those words students can type up to that point.

Enrichment ● Lesson 3

Type each line 2 times.

A. NEW-KEY REINFORCEMENT

O 1 roost hotfoot solon forefoot loose offshoot odors
R 2 errs rater refer retro rotor harder roster resort
H 3 hardhats hasheesh hosanna hotshots rehashed flesh

O 4 nonfood shook forenoon stood torso onlooker hoots
R 5 darter terser horror roller eraser roarer errands
H 6 sheathed shoehorn aha thrasher handshake thrasher

O 7 shoot foothold forsooth noose stool rodeo tootles
R 8 narrator restorer tearjerker referral northerners
H 9 harshness horseshoe hotheaded shorthand threshold

O R H 10 rho ashore hoorah hero hereto shorts hoar hoarser
O R H 11 hoer holder hora horn honker forth horned shofars
O R H 12 frosh throes froth honor heron horror hoard honer

Type each line 2 times.
Do not type the colored vertical lines.

B. SHORT PHRASES

13 a loose shade|eats a short noodle|the rose thorns
14 a tattletale|she sat here|he often jostled a jerk
15 the rest of the lesson|thanks for the short looks

16 the oddest tattoos|those stolen forks|do not jerk
17 the shore floods|she flossed her teeth|jot a note
18 the earth shook hard|had a look|a tenth of a foot

Type each line 2 times.

C. CLAUSES

19 she shared her salad at the hotel near the shore;
20 three deer ran to the dark oak tree near the ark;
21 she had then also looked at the other ten horses;

22 she set all of the stolen art on that tall shelf;
23 take a seat near the dark settee and talk to her;
24 the teal sandals on her feet had soon fallen off;

25 the loose earth on the north and east had fallen;
26 ask her not to take the nonfat food to the stall;
27 the senator held a safe seat and soon left there;

Enrichment ● Lesson 3   **13**

Individualized Skillbuilding
In every lesson

Warmups at the start of each lesson comprise 3 lines. Line 1 is an alphabetic sentence to review all reaches; Line 2 practices a particular type of reach; Line 3 contains easy words to help build speed.

Skillbuilding (building straight-copy speed and accuracy) is built into *every lesson*—15'–20' of *individualized* skill-building routines.

Each student always practices on the type of drill that is appropriate for him or her and for which the **individualized** goals are challenging—but attainable.

The **timed writings** in every even-numbered lesson are controlled for difficulty, contain all letters of the alphabet, and are the exact length needed to achieve that lesson's speed goal.

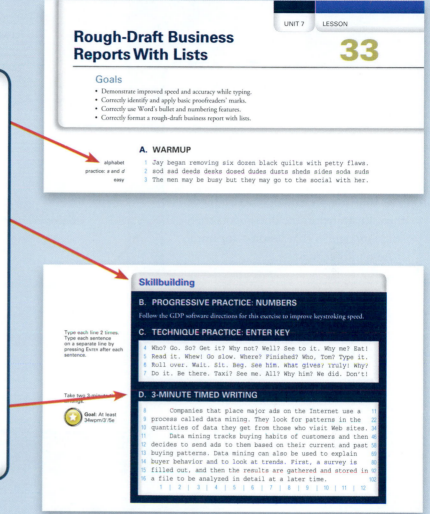

UNIT 7   LESSON

Rough-Draft Business Reports With Lists

33

Goals
- Demonstrate improved speed and accuracy while typing.
- Correctly identify and apply basic proofreaders' marks.
- Correctly use Word's bullet and numbering features.
- Correctly format a rough-draft business report with lists.

A. WARMUP

alphabet   1   Jay began removing six dozen black quilts with petty flaws.
practice: *s and d*   2   sod sad deeds desks dosed dudes dusts sheds sides soda suds
easy   3   The men may be busy but they may go to the social with her.

Skillbuilding

B. PROGRESSIVE PRACTICE: NUMBERS
Follow the GDP software directions for this exercise to improve keystroking speed.

C. TECHNIQUE PRACTICE: ENTER KEY

Type each line 2 times. Type each sentence on a separate line by pressing ENTER after each sentence.

4   Who? Go. So? Get it? Why not? Well? See to it. Why me? Eat!
5   Read it. Whew! Go slow. Where? Finished? Who, Tom? Type it.
6   Roll over. Wait. Sit. Beg. See him. What gives? Truly! Why?
7   Do it. Be there. Taxi? See me. All? Why him? We did. Don't!

D. 3-MINUTE TIMED WRITING

Take two 3-minute timed writings.

⭐ Goal: At least 34wpm/3'/5e

8   Companies that place major ads on the Internet use a   11
9   process called data mining. They look for patterns in the   22
10   quantities of data they get from those who visit Web sites.   34
11   Data mining tracks buying habits of customers and then   46
12   decides to send ads to them based on their current and past   58
13   buying patterns. Data mining can also be used to explain   69
14   buyer behavior and to look at trends. First, a survey is   80
15   filled out, and then the results are gathered and stored in   92
16   a file to be analyzed in detail at a later time.   102
   1 | 2 | 3 | 4 | 5 | 6 | 7 | 8 | 9 | 10 | 11 | 12

Language Arts
A critical document processing skill

Language arts (punctuation rules, usage, proofreading, composing, and spelling) are systematically covered. Short, easy-to-grasp exercises are incorporated throughout Lessons 21–120 with increasing difficulty.

The rules are presented, practiced, and then illustrated in the documents that students type in that lesson—for immediate reinforcement.

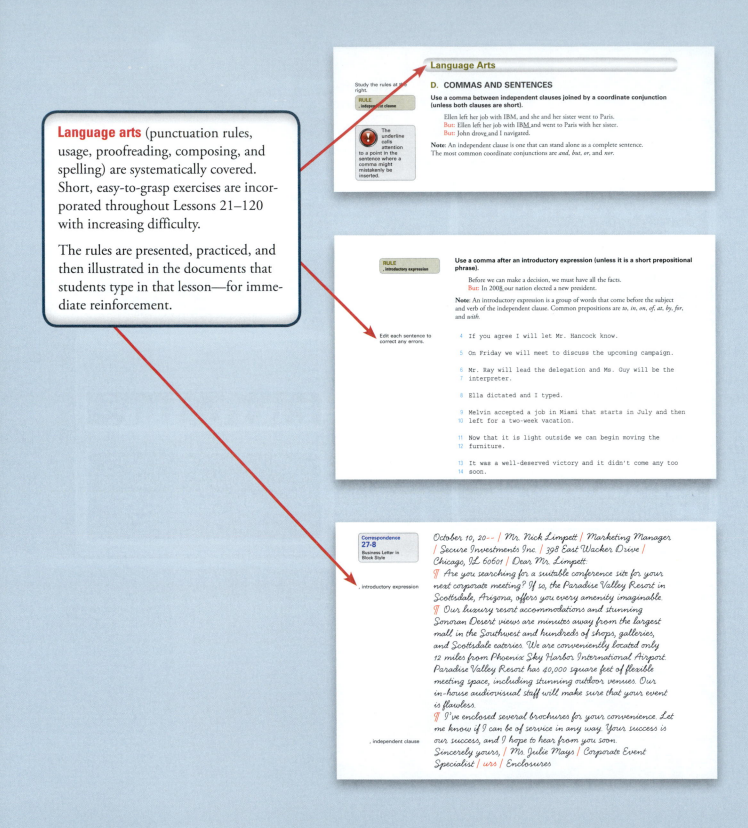

Language Arts

Study the rules at the right.

RULE
, independent clause

The underline calls attention to a point in the sentence where a comma might mistakenly be inserted.

D. COMMAS AND SENTENCES

Use a comma between independent clauses joined by a coordinate conjunction (unless both clauses are short).

Ellen left her job with IBM, and she and her sister went to Paris.
But: Ellen left her job with IBM and went to Paris with her sister.
But: John drove and I navigated.

Note: An independent clause is one that can stand alone as a complete sentence. The most common coordinate conjunctions are *and, but, or,* and *nor.*

RULE
, introductory expression

Use a comma after an introductory expression (unless it is a short prepositional phrase).

Before we can make a decision, we must have all the facts.
But: In 2008 our nation elected a new president.

Note: An introductory expression is a group of words that come before the subject and verb of the independent clause. Common prepositions are *to, in, on, of, at, by, for,* and *with.*

Edit each sentence to correct any errors.

4 If you agree I will let Mr. Hancock know.

5 On Friday we will meet to discuss the upcoming campaign.

6 Mr. Ray will lead the delegation and Ms. Guy will be the
7 interpreter.

8 Ella dictated and I typed.

9 Melvin accepted a job in Miami that starts in July and then
10 left for a two-week vacation.

11 Now that it is light outside we can begin moving the
12 furniture.

13 It was a well-deserved victory and it didn't come any too
14 soon.

Correspondence
27-8
Business Letter in Block Style

, introductory expression

, independent clause

October 10, 20-- / Mr. Nick Limpett / Marketing Manager / Secure Investments Inc. / 398 East Wacker Drive / Chicago, IL 60601 / Dear Mr. Limpett:
¶ Are you searching for a suitable conference site for your next corporate meeting? If so, the Paradise Valley Resort in Scottsdale, Arizona, offers you every amenity imaginable.
¶ Our luxury resort accommodations and stunning Sonoran Desert views are minutes away from the largest mall in the Southwest and hundreds of shops, galleries, and Scottsdale eateries. We are conveniently located only 12 miles from Phoenix Sky Harbor International Airport. Paradise Valley Resort has 40,000 square feet of flexible meeting space, including stunning outdoor venues. Our in-house audiovisual staff will make sure that your event is flawless.
¶ I've enclosed several brochures for your convenience. Let me know if I can be of service in any way. Your success is our success, and I hope to hear from you soon.
Sincerely yours, / Ms. Julie Mays / Corporate Event Specialist / urs / Enclosures

New! Expanded Ten-Key Practice

Students learn to touch-type the entire ten-key pad—a frequent job requirement. After Lesson 20, a new **Ten-Key Numeric Keypad** supplementary lesson teaches the touch typing of both the number keys *and the arithmetic operators* (+ - * and /)—for a total of 55 new lines of drills.

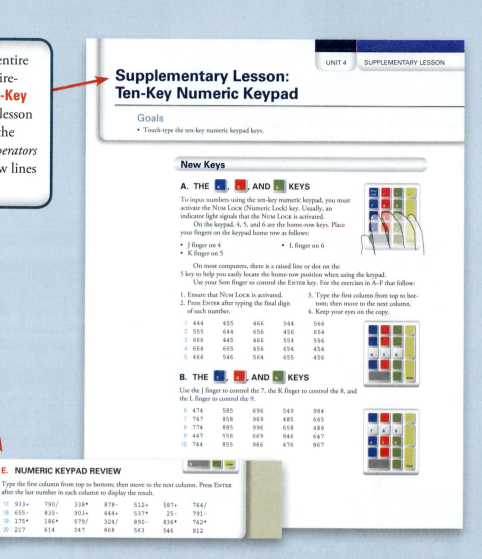

Word Processing Commands
Introduced on a *need-to-know* basis

Word processing commands are introduced when they are needed to format a particular job (in this lesson, students need to learn the Italic and Underline commands).

Students are referred to the corresponding lesson in the *Word Manual*, which contains step-by-step directions, with screen shots and practice exercises so that students don't get lost.

When students finish the practice exercises in the *Word Manual*, they are referred back to the text.

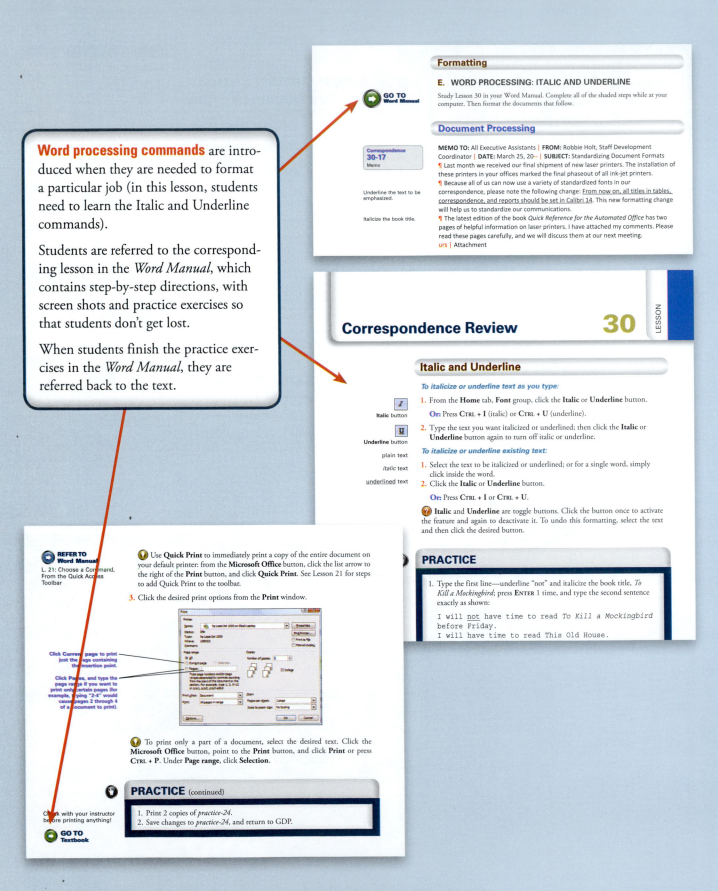

Formatting

E. WORD PROCESSING: ITALIC AND UNDERLINE

GO TO Word Manual

Study Lesson 30 in your Word Manual. Complete all of the shaded steps while at your computer. Then format the documents that follow.

Document Processing

Correspondence 30-17 Memo

Underline the text to be emphasized.

Italicize the book title.

MEMO TO: All Executive Assistants | **FROM:** Robbie Holt, Staff Development Coordinator | **DATE:** March 25, 20-- | **SUBJECT:** Standardizing Document Formats

¶ Last month we received our final shipment of new laser printers. The installation of these printers in your offices marked the final phaseout of all ink-jet printers.

¶ Because all of us can now use a variety of standardized fonts in our correspondence, please note the following change: From now on, all titles in tables, correspondence, and reports should be set in Calibri 14. This new formatting change will help us to standardize our communications.

¶ The latest edition of the book *Quick Reference for the Automated Office* has two pages of helpful information on laser printers. I have attached my comments. Please read these pages carefully, and we will discuss them at our next meeting.

urs | Attachment

Correspondence Review   30   LESSON

Italic and Underline

To italicize or underline text as you type:

I Italic button

1. From the **Home** tab, **Font** group, click the **Italic** or **Underline** button.

   Or: Press **CTRL + I** (italic) or **CTRL + U** (underline).

U Underline button

2. Type the text you want italicized or underlined; then click the **Italic** or **Underline** button again to turn off italic or underline.

plain text
italic text
underlined text

To italicize or underline existing text:

1. Select the text to be italicized or underlined; or for a single word, simply click inside the word.

2. Click the **Italic** or **Underline** button.

   Or: Press **CTRL + I** or **CTRL + U**.

❓ Italic and Underline are toggle buttons. Click the button once to activate the feature and again to deactivate it. To undo this formatting, select the text and then click the desired button.

PRACTICE

1. Type the first line—underline "not" and italicize the book title, *To Kill a Mockingbird*; press **ENTER** 1 time, and type the second sentence exactly as shown:

```
I will not have time to read To Kill a Mockingbird
before Friday.
I will have time to read This Old House.
```

REFER TO Word Manual

L. 21: Choose a Command, From the Quick Access Toolbar

💡 Use **Quick Print** to immediately print a copy of the entire document on your default printer: from the **Microsoft Office** button, click the list arrow to the right of the **Print** button, and click **Quick Print**. See Lesson 21 for steps to add Quick Print to the toolbar.

3. Click the desired print options from the **Print** window.

Click **Current page** to print just the page containing the insertion point.

Click **Pages**, and type the page range if you want to print only certain pages (for example, typing "2-4" would cause pages 2 through 4 of a document to print).

💡 To print only a part of a document, select the desired text. Click the **Microsoft Office** button, point to the **Print** button, and click **Print** or press **CTRL + P**. Under **Page range**, click **Selection**.

PRACTICE (continued)

1. Print 2 copies of *practice-24*.
2. Save changes to *practice-24*, and return to GDP.

Check with your instructor before printing anything!

GO TO Textbook

GDP Instructor Help
Right where you need it!

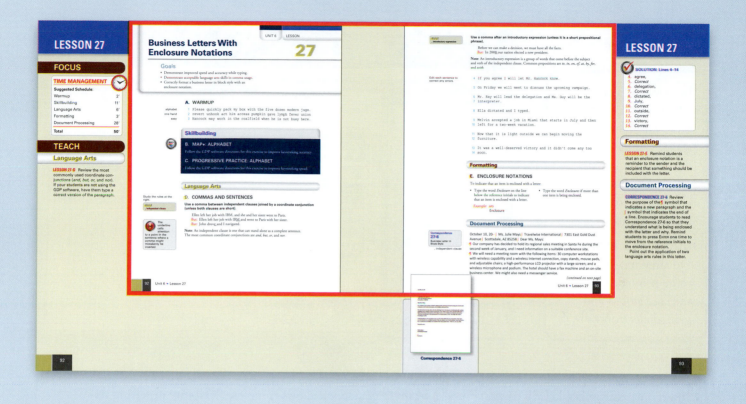

The ***Instructor Wraparound Edition (IWE)*** offers lesson plans and reduced-size student pages (shown in the red border above) to enhance classroom instruction. In addition to a mini-methods section at the front of the *IWE*, the side and bottom panels on each lesson page contain:

- Suggested times for each lesson part

- Miniature copies of the solutions for the documents students type in that lesson

- Solutions to language arts activities

- Marginal teaching notes—right where they are needed

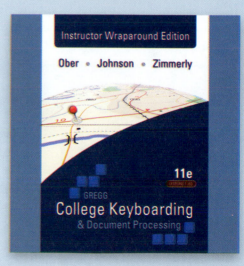

No More Grading Papers!
New! GDP now scores both keystroking and *formatting* errors

Instructors decide whether to have GDP automatically assign a grade to each document—based on parameters they choose—or to assign a grade manually.

GDP goes green.
Documents don't need to be printed because they are stored and graded electronically.

GDP GREGG
College Keyboarding & Document Processing

Help ? Close X
Joe Student

Lessons | Skillbuilding | MAP+ | Timed Writings | Language Arts | Reference Manual | My GDP

Basic Business Documents

- ✓ **Lesson 31** One-Page Business Reports
- ⚠ **Lesson 32** Multipage Business Reports
  - ✓ 32A: Warmup
  - ✓ 32B: Sustained Practice: Alternate-Hand Words
  - ✓ 32C: 3-Minute Timed Writing
  - ✓ 32D: Multipage Business Reports
  - ✓ 32E: Business Reports with Paragraph Headings
  - ✓ 32F: Word Processing: Page Number, Page Break, and Widow/Orphan Control
  - ✓ Report 32-3: Business Report
  - Report 32-4: Business Report
- **Lesson 33** Rough-Draft Business Reports with Lists
- **Lesson 34** Multipage Academic Reports with Lists
- **Lesson 35** More Rough-Draft Reports

Report 32-3: Business Report

1 Start
2 Review and Submit
3 View Results

Time Spent: 12:32		Typing Errors: 6	Details
Formatting Errors: 5			Details

Formatting Change	Error
Title Line 1: Not bold	1
Byline: Font change (unnecessary)	1
Date: Font size change (unnecessary)	1
Paragraph 1: Alignment change (unnecessary)	1
Side Heading 1: Not bold	1

New! The customizable **GPS (Grade Posting System)** gradebook allows complete flexibility in setting up grades—with an easy-to-use, intuitive interface. Students can check their current average at any point in the school term, and instructors can save the gradebook in a comma-delimited format for uploading to Excel or to learning management systems (LMS) such as Blackboard or Angel.

GDP GREGG
College Keyboarding & Document Processing

Signed in as **Torger Wuellner** (sign out)
Last sign in was **Tuesday, December 15 2009, 3:10 PM**

? Help

GPS

USERS
My Account
Message Center
Instructors
Students
Classes

CONTENT
Resources

RESULTS
GPS

ADMINISTRATION
Settings

SECURED BY GeoTrust

Student	Word Proc. Tests	Custom Timed Writings	Attendance	Course Grade
Bruiser, Donald (Dbruiser)	85%	100%	35 / 35	B
Daze, Matthew (Mdaze)	85%	95%	34 / 35	C
Gamin, Ben (Bgamin)	95%	90%	33 / 35	A
Hannah, Jared (1983575932)	75%	78%	31 / 35	C
James, Emily (7810258615)	86%	80%	35 / 35	B
Jones, Kayla (Kjones)	95%	100%	35 / 35	B
Kumar, Raheem (rkumar)	82%	72%	29 / 35	B
Lancaster, Richard (1835750667)	89%	77%	30 / 35	C
Mercardo, Eduardo (emercardo)	85%	98%	35 / 35	B
Smith, Jonathan (JSmith22)	78%	88%	35 / 35	B
Smith, Angela (ASmith)	80%	100%	30 / 35	D
Zhao, Da-Xia (dzhao)	77%	92%	30 / 35	C

Contents

PART 1
The Alphabet, Number, and Symbol Keys

SKILLBUILDING

Preface

Gregg College Keyboarding & Document Processing is a multicomponent instructional program designed to give the student and the instructor a high degree of flexibility and a high degree of success in meeting their respective goals. The textbook is offered in several volumes: *Lessons 1–20, Lessons 1–60, Lessons 61–120,* and *Lessons 1–120.* The GDP software is a Web-delivered, PC-compatible program providing complete lesson-by-lesson instruction for each of the 120 text lessons. The document processing *Word Manual,* used in conjunction with the textbook for Lessons 21–120, teaches the document processing skills needed to create efficient business documents using Microsoft Word.

The Kit Format

For student and instructor convenience, the core components of this instructional system—the textbook, the *Word Manual,* and the Gregg College Keyboarding & Document Processing (GDP) software—are available in a variety of kit formats.

Kit 1: Lessons 1–60 This kit, designed for the first keyboarding course, provides the Lessons 1–60 textbook, the *Word Manual,* and an access card to the GDP software. Since this kit is designed for the beginning student, its major objectives are to develop touch control of the keyboard and proper keyboarding techniques, to build basic speed and accuracy, and to provide practice in applying those basic skills to the formatting of e-mails, reports, letters, memos, tables, and other kinds of personal and business communications.

Kit 2: Lessons 61–120 This kit, designed for the second course, provides the Lessons 61–120 textbook, the *Word Manual,* and an access card to the GDP software. This course continues the development of basic keyboarding skills and emphasizes the formatting of various kinds of business correspondence, reports, tables, electronic forms, and desktop publishing projects from arranged, unarranged, handwritten, and rough-draft sources.

Kit 3: Lessons 1–120 This kit, designed for both the first and second course, provides the Lessons 1–120 textbook, the *Word Manual,* and an access card to the GDP software.

Kit 4: Lessons 1–20 This kit, designed for shorter keyboarding courses, provides the Lessons 1–20 text and an access card to the GDP software.

Supporting Materials

Gregg College Keyboarding & Document Processing offers the following instructional materials:

- The special *Instructor Wraparound Edition (IWE)* offers lesson plans and reduced-size student pages to enhance classroom instruction. Distance-learning tips, instructional methodology, adult learner strategies, and special needs features also are included in this wraparound edition. New to this edition are miniature solutions for each document the students type; they are shown in the margins of the IWE.
- The *Tests and Solutions Manual* provides solution keys for all of the formatting in Lessons 25–120 in addition to objective tests and alternative document processing tests for each part.

What's New in the 11th Edition Text?

New-Key Introduction (Lessons 1–20)

- A new Enrichment page has been added to each of the first 20 lessons—for additional practice and faster development of touch-typing skills.
- MAP+ (Misstroke Analysis and Prescription) can now be used beginning with Lesson 1, thus providing unlimited new practice drills for each of the new-key lessons.
- A new supplementary lesson, Ten-Key Numeric Keypad, follows Lesson 20; it teaches the touch typing of both the number keys and arithmetic operators (+, -, /, and *), with 55 new drill lines.
- Only 3 new keys are introduced in each lesson (instead of 4)—to provide more intensive practice on each new key; all keys are still introduced in Lessons 1–20.
- The order in which new keys are introduced has been refined to balance the workload between each hand and to take into consideration how frequently keys are used. For example, in previous editions, the hyphen key was introduced early (in Lesson 6) because students used it for manual word division. With Word's automatic hyphenation feature, students don't use this key as much anymore, and the hyphen is now introduced in Lesson 11.

Skillbuilding

- MAP+ now provides an analysis and prescription of the number and symbol keys (previously, only alphabetic reaches were included). Because of this, (a) Diagnostic Practice: Symbols and Punctuation and (b) Diagnostic Practice: Numbers have been removed.
- Every Warmup exercise has been revised. Line 1 of each Warmup is now an alphabetic sentence to review all reaches, Line 2 practices a particular type of reach, and Line 3 contains easy words to build speed.

Document Processing

- Formatting correspondence (new Unit 6) is now introduced before formatting reports (new Unit 7).
- The formatting of bulleted/numbered lists in Lesson 33 and table column headings in Lesson 38 has been simplified.
- More e-mail messages are included with added coverage of formatting, such as bulleted lists, tables, and attachments.
- Eleven new Word commands are introduced: Zoom (L. 24), Widow/Orphan Control (L. 32), Table—Align Bottom (L. 38), AutoCorrect—Hyperlink (L. 49), Bookmarks and Hyperlinks (L. 89), Cover Page—Insert (L. 90), Table—Tab (L. 92), Page Color (L. 107), Mail Merge (L. 113–115), Style Set—Word 2007 (Appendix A), and PDF Format (Appendix C).

- The electronic resume in Lesson 52 (which is not being used much anymore) has been replaced by job-interviewing documents.
- The Web project in Unit 23 has been changed from creating a company home page to (a) creating an online resume and (b) introducing Mail Merge.
- Each lesson of the *Instructor's Wraparound Edition* now displays a miniature solution for each document students type in that lesson.

Introduction to the Student

Starting a Lesson

Each lesson begins with the goals for that lesson. Read the goals carefully so that you understand the purpose of your practice. In the example at the right (from Lesson 26), the goals for the lesson are to type at least 30 wpm (words per minute) on a 3-minute timed writing with no more than 5 uncorrected errors and to correctly format a business letter in block style with standard punctuation.

Building Straight-Copy Skill

Warmups. Each lesson begins with a Warmup that reinforces learned alphabet, number, and/or symbol keys; practices specific reaches; and builds speed.

Skillbuilding. The Skillbuilding portion of each lesson includes a variety of drills to individualize your keyboarding speed and accuracy development. Instructions for completing the drills are always provided beside each activity.

Additional Skillbuilding drills are included in the back of the textbook and on the GDP correlated software. These drills are intended to help you meet your individual goals.

Measuring Straight-Copy Skill

Straight-copy skill is measured in wpm. All timed writings are the exact length needed to meet the speed goal for the lesson. If you finish a timed writing before time is up, you have automatically reached your speed goal for the lesson.

Counting Errors. Specific criteria are used for counting errors. The GDP software counts an error when

1. Any stroke is incorrect.
2. Any punctuation after a word is incorrect or omitted. The word before the punctuation is counted as incorrect.
3. The spacing after a word or after its punctuation is incorrect. The word is counted as incorrect.
4. A letter or word is omitted or repeated.
5. A direction about spacing, indenting, and so on, is not followed.
6. Words are transposed.

(**Note:** Only one error is counted for each word, no matter how many errors it may contain. The GDP correlated software automatically proofreads your copy and marks any errors for you.)

Determining Speed. To compute your typing speed in wpm, the GDP software counts every 5 strokes, including spaces, as 1 "word." Horizontal word scales below an activity divide lines into 5-stroke words. Vertical word scales to the right of an activity show the number of words in each line cumulatively totaled.

For example, the illustration that follows is for a 2-minute timed writing. If you complete line 30, you have typed 11 words. If you complete line 31, you have typed 22 words. Use the bottom word scale to determine the word count of a partial line. Add that number to the cumulative total for the last complete line. The GDP correlated software automatically computes your wpm speed for you.

Goals

- Type at least 30wpm/3'/5e by touch.
- Correctly format a business letter in block style with standard punctuation.

Take two 2-minute
timed writings.

Goal: At least
19wpm/2'/5e

```
30          Zachary just paid for six seats and quit because he      11
31   could not get the views he required near the middle of the      22
32   field. In August he thinks he may go to the ticket office      34
33   to purchase tickets.                                            38
        1  |  2  |  3  |  4  |  5  |  6  |  7  |  8  |  9  |  10  |  11  |  12
```

Correcting Errors

You will make numerous errors while you are learning the keyboard; do not be overly concerned about them. Errors will decrease as you become familiar with the keyboard. Error-correction settings in the GDP software determine whether you can correct errors in timed writings and drills. Consult your instructor for error-correction guidelines.

To correct an error, press Backspace (shown as ← on some keyboards) to delete the incorrect character(s). Then type the correct character(s).

If you notice an error on a different line, use the up, down, left, or right arrows to move the insertion point immediately to the left or right of the error. Press Backspace to delete a character to the left of the insertion point or Delete to delete a character to the right of the insertion point.

Typing Technique

Correct position at the keyboard enables you to type with greater speed and accuracy and with less fatigue. When typing for a long period, rest your eyes occasionally by looking away from the screen. Change position, walk around, or stretch when your muscles feel tired. Making such movements and adjustments may help prevent your body from becoming too tired. In addition, long-term bodily damage, such as carpal tunnel syndrome, can be prevented.

Follow these ergonomic principles when typing:

Workstation

1. Position your chair so that your upper and lower legs form a greater-than-90-degree angle and your lower back is supported, with your knees slightly lower than your hips.
2. Position your text on either side of the monitor as close to the monitor vertically and horizontally as possible.
3. Position the mouse on a pad next to and at the same height as your keyboard.
4. Tilt the top of the monitor slightly away from you and slightly farther than an arm's length from you.

Position at the Keyboard

5. Center your body in front of the keyboard.
6. Sit slightly reclined, with your lower back touching the back of the chair and your feet flat on the floor.
7. Keep your elbows close to your body in a relaxed position.
8. Curve your fingers naturally over the home-row position, with the back of your hands at the same angle as the keyboard.
9. Move the mouse with your whole arm—not just your wrist.

Keystroking

10. Operate all keys by touch, using the correct fingers.
11. Keep your eyes on the copy most of the time while typing.

12. Keep your forearms at a slight downward slant and raise your hands slightly when typing so that your wrists do not touch the keyboard.
13. Make quick, light strokes, returning your fingers immediately to the home-row position or moving to the next position after each stroke.

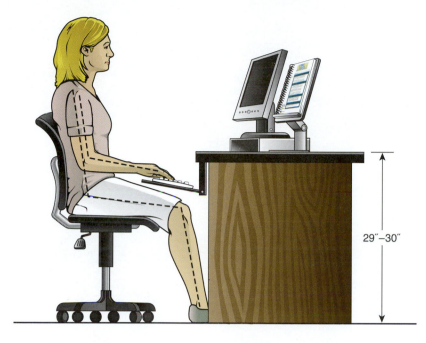

Tension-Reducing Exercises

A variety of government and health sources recommend the following exercises for computer users. Perform one exercise from each group, hold each position for three seconds, and repeat each exercise three times.

Neck

1. Look forward and slowly tilt your head as far to the left as possible. Then slowly tilt your head as far to the right as possible.
2. Slowly tilt your head forward until your chin rests on your chest. Then slowly tilt your head as far back as possible.

Shoulders

3. Roll your shoulders forward in a large circle. Then roll your shoulders backward in a large circle.
4. Extend both arms out to your side. Then slowly stretch them toward your back and squeeze your shoulder blades together. Finally, slowly bring your arms forward and touch the tops of your hands together in front of you.

Back

5. Place both hands behind your head, and slowly stretch your upper body backward. Then slowly bend all the way forward, stretching your arms toward the floor.
6. While seated, grab your left knee with both hands and slowly pull your leg in toward your body. Then repeat with your right knee.

Eyes

7. Close your eyes tightly. Then open them as wide as you can, blinking rapidly.
8. Follow the 20/20/20 rule: every 20 minutes, stare at an object 20 feet away for 20 seconds.

Reference Manual

Reference Manual

A. MAJOR PARTS OF A COMPUTER SYSTEM

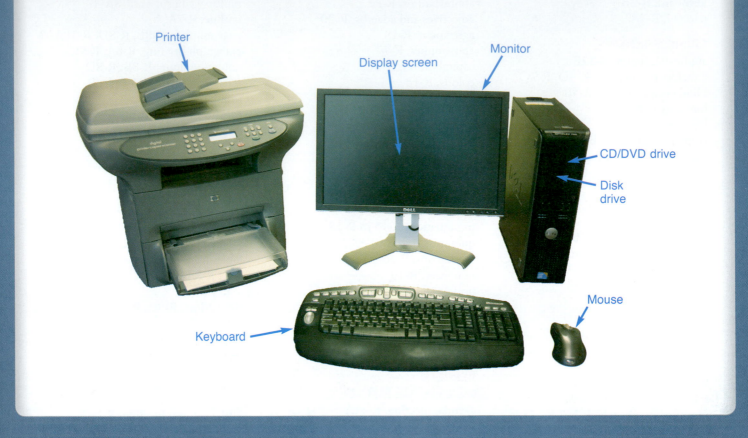

Printer

Display screen

Monitor

CD/DVD drive

Disk drive

Mouse

Keyboard

B. THE COMPUTER KEYBOARD

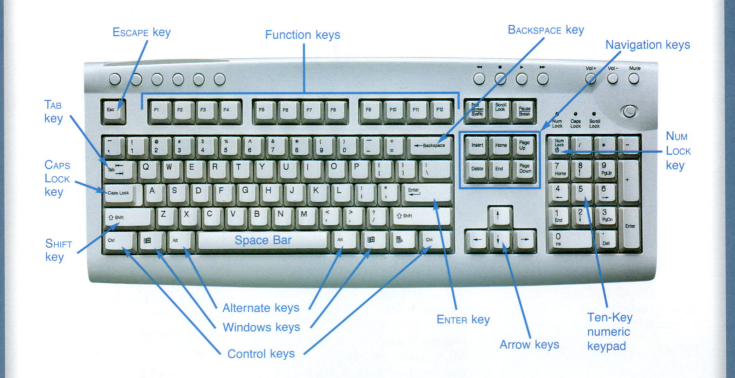

ESCAPE key

Function keys

BACKSPACE key

Navigation keys

TAB key

NUM LOCK key

CAPS LOCK key

SHIFT key

Alternate keys

Windows keys

Control keys

ENTER key

Arrow keys

Ten-Key numeric keypad

Reference Manual

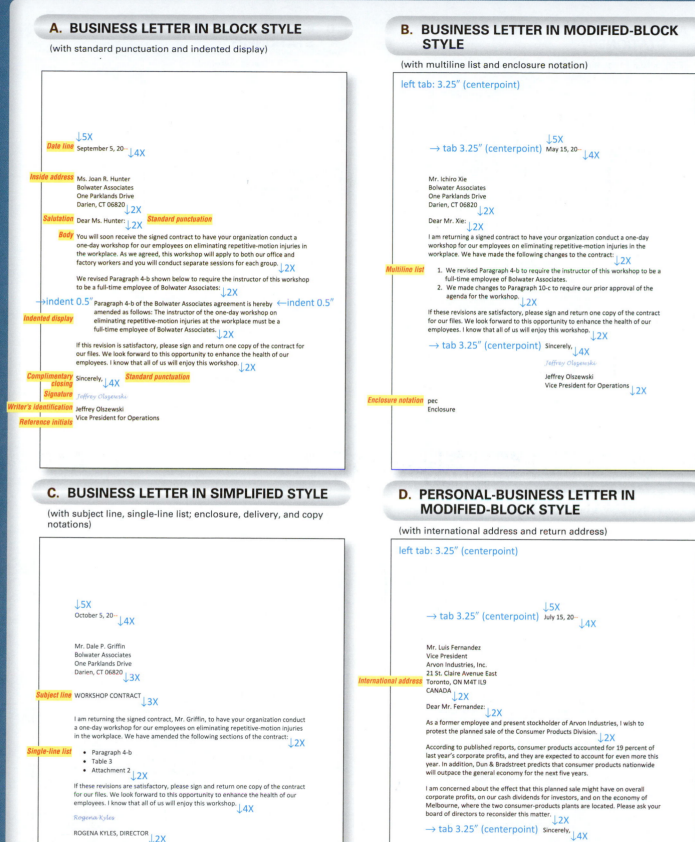

A. BUSINESS LETTER IN BLOCK STYLE

(with standard punctuation and indented display)

Date line ↓5X
September 5, 20-- ↓4X

Inside address Ms. Joan R. Hunter
Bolwater Associates
One Parklands Drive
Darien, CT 06820 ↓2X

Salutation Dear Ms. Hunter: ↓2X **Standard punctuation**

Body You will soon receive the signed contract to have your organization conduct a one-day workshop for our employees on eliminating repetitive-motion injuries in the workplace. As we agreed, this workshop will apply to both our office and factory workers and you will conduct separate sessions for each group. ↓2X

We revised Paragraph 4-b shown below to require the instructor of this workshop to be a full-time employee of Bolwater Associates. ↓2X

→indent 0.5" Paragraph 4-b of the Bolwater Associates agreement is hereby ←indent 0.5"

Indented display amended as follows: The instructor of the one-day workshop on eliminating repetitive-motion injuries at the workplace must be a full-time employee of Bolwater Associates. ↓2X

If this revision is satisfactory, please sign and return one copy of the contract for our files. We look forward to this opportunity to enhance the health of our employees. I know that all of us will enjoy this workshop. ↓2X

Complimentary closing Sincerely, ↓4X **Standard punctuation**

Signature *Jeffrey Olszewski*

Writer's identification Jeffrey Olszewski
Vice President for Operations

Reference initials

B. BUSINESS LETTER IN MODIFIED-BLOCK STYLE

(with multiline list and enclosure notation)

left tab: 3.25" (centerpoint)

→ tab 3.25" (centerpoint) May 15, 20-- ↓5X ↓4X

Mr. Ichiro Xie
Bolwater Associates
One Parklands Drive
Darien, CT 06820 ↓2X

Dear Mr. Xie: ↓2X

I am returning a signed contract to have your organization conduct a one-day workshop for our employees on eliminating repetitive-motion injuries in the workplace. We have made the following changes to the contract: ↓2X

Multiline list
1. We revised Paragraph 4-b to require the instructor of this workshop to be a full-time employee of Bolwater Associates.
2. We made changes to Paragraph 10-c to require our prior approval of the agenda for the workshop. ↓2X

If these revisions are satisfactory, please sign and return one copy of the contract for our files. We look forward to this opportunity to enhance the health of our employees. I know that all of us will enjoy this workshop. ↓2X

→ tab 3.25" (centerpoint) Sincerely, ↓4X

Jeffrey Olszewski

Jeffrey Olszewski
Vice President for Operations ↓2X

Enclosure notation pec
Enclosure

C. BUSINESS LETTER IN SIMPLIFIED STYLE

(with subject line, single-line list; enclosure, delivery, and copy notations)

↓5X
October 5, 20-- ↓4X

Mr. Dale P. Griffin
Bolwater Associates
One Parklands Drive
Darien, CT 06820 ↓3X

Subject line WORKSHOP CONTRACT ↓3X

I am returning the signed contract, Mr. Griffin, to have your organization conduct a one-day workshop for our employees on eliminating repetitive-motion injuries in the workplace. We have amended the following sections of the contract: ↓2X

Single-line list
- Paragraph 4-b
- Table 3
- Attachment 2 ↓2X

If these revisions are satisfactory, please sign and return one copy of the contract for our files. We look forward to this opportunity to enhance the health of our employees. I know that all of us will enjoy this workshop. ↓4X

Rogena Kyles

ROGENA KYLES, DIRECTOR ↓2X

iww
Enclosure notation Enclosure
Delivery notation By e-mail
Copy notation c: Legal Department

D. PERSONAL-BUSINESS LETTER IN MODIFIED-BLOCK STYLE

(with international address and return address)

left tab: 3.25" (centerpoint)

→ tab 3.25" (centerpoint) July 15, 20-- ↓5X ↓4X

Mr. Luis Fernandez
Vice President
Arvon Industries, Inc.
21 St. Claire Avenue East
International address Toronto, ON M4T IL9
CANADA ↓2X

Dear Mr. Fernandez: ↓2X

As a former employee and present stockholder of Arvon Industries, I wish to protest the planned sale of the Consumer Products Division. ↓2X

According to published reports, consumer products accounted for 19 percent of last year's corporate profits, and they are expected to account for even more this year. In addition, Dun & Bradstreet predicts that consumer products nationwide will outpace the general economy for the next five years. ↓2X

I am concerned about the effect that this planned sale might have on overall corporate profits, on our cash dividends for investors, and on the economy of Melbourne, where the two consumer-products plants are located. Please ask your board of directors to reconsider this matter. ↓2X

→ tab 3.25" (centerpoint) Sincerely, ↓4X

Jeanine Ford

Jeanine Ford
Return address 901 East Benson, Apt. 3
Fort Lauderdale, FL 33301
U.S.A.

Reference Manual

A. BUSINESS LETTER ON EXECUTIVE STATIONERY

(7.25" × 10.5"; 1" side margins; with delivery notation)

↓5X
July 18, 20-- ↓4X

Mr. Rodney Eastwood
BBL Resources
523 Northern Ridge
Fayetteville, PA 17222 ↓2X

Dear Rodney: ↓2X

I see no reason why we should continue to consider the locality around Geraldton for our new plant. Even though the desirability of this site from an economic view is undeniable, there is not sufficient housing readily available for our workers. ↓2X

In trying to control urban growth, the city has been turning down the building permits for much new housing or placing so many restrictions on foreign investment as to make it too expensive.

Please continue to seek out other areas of exploration where we might form a joint partnership. ↓2X

Sincerely, ↓4X

Jennifer Gwatkin

Jennifer Gwatkin, Director ↓2X

mme
By fax

Delivery notation

B. BUSINESS LETTER ON HALF-PAGE STATIONERY

(5.5" × 8.5"; 0.75" side margins)

↓4X
July 18, 20-- ↓4X

Mr. Aristeo Olivas
BBL Resources
52A Northern Ridge
Fayetteville, PA 17222 ↓2X

Dear Aristeo ↓2X

We should discontinue considering Geraldton for our new plant. Housing is not readily available.

Please seek out other areas of exploration where we might someday form a joint partnership. ↓2X

Sincerely, ↓4X

Chimere Jones

Chimere Jones, Director ↓2X

adk

C. BUSINESS LETTER FORMATTED FOR A WINDOW ENVELOPE

(with open punctuation)

↓5X
July 18, 20-- ↓3X

Ms. Reinalda Guerrero
BBL Resources
52A Northern Ridge
Fayetteville, PA 17222 ↓3X

Dear Ms. Guerrero ↓2X *Open punctuation*

I see no reason why we should even continue to consider the locality around Geraldton for our new plant. Even though the desirability of this site from an economic view is undeniable, there is insufficient housing readily available for our workers. ↓2X

In trying to control urban growth, the city has been turning down the building permits for new housing or placing so many restrictions on foreign investment as to make it too expensive.

Please continue to seek out other areas of exploration where we might form a joint partnership. ↓2X

Sincerely ↓4X *Open punctuation*

Augustus Mays

Augustus Mays
Vice President for Operations ↓2X

woc

D. MEMO

(with ruled table, left- and right-aligned columns, and attachment notation)

↓5X →tab

MEMO TO: Nancy Price, Executive Vice President ↓2X

FROM: Arlyn J. Bunch, Operations *ajb*

DATE: July 18, 20--

SUBJECT: New Plant Site ↓2X

As you can see from the attached letter, I've informed BBL Resources that I see no reason why we should continue to consider the locality around Geraldton for our new plant. Even though the desirability of this site from an economic standpoint is undeniable, there is insufficient housing available. In fact, as of June 25, the number of appropriate single-family houses listed for sale within a 25-mile radius of Geraldton was as follows: ↓2X

Ruled table

Agent	Units
Belle Real Estate	123
Castleton Homes	11
Red Carpet	9
Geraldton Homes	5

↓1X

In addition, in trying to control urban growth, Geraldton has been either turning down building permits for new housing or placing excessive restrictions on them. Because of this deficiency of housing for our employees, we have no choice but to look elsewhere. ↓2X

woc

Attachment notation Attachment

Reference Manual

A. MULTIPAGE BUSINESS LETTER

(page 1; with on-arrival notation, international address, subject line, and boxed table)

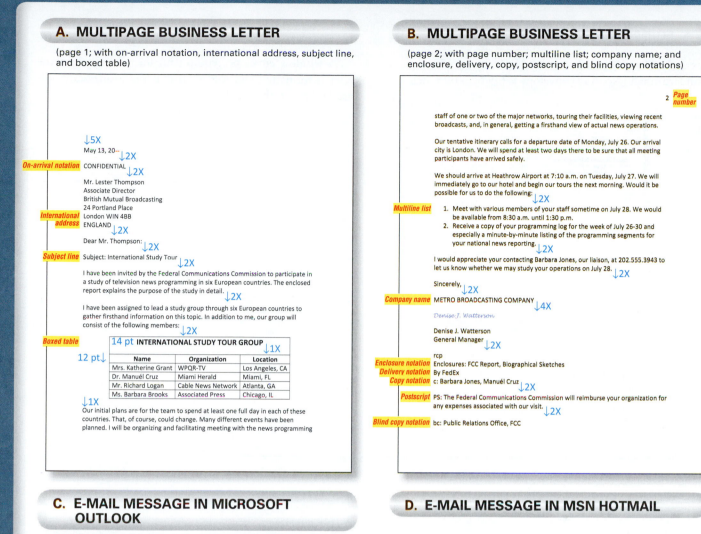

↓5X

May 13, 20--
↓2X
On-arrival notation CONFIDENTIAL
↓2X
Mr. Lester Thompson
Associate Director
British Mutual Broadcasting
24 Portland Place
International address London WIN 4BB
ENGLAND
↓2X
Dear Mr. Thompson:
↓2X
Subject line Subject: International Study Tour
↓2X
I have been invited by the Federal Communications Commission to participate in a study of television news programming in six European countries. The enclosed report explains the purpose of the study in detail.
↓2X
I have been assigned to lead a study group through six European countries to gather firsthand information on this topic. In addition to me, our group will consist of the following members:
↓2X

Boxed table

14 pt INTERNATIONAL STUDY TOUR GROUP		
Name	**Organization**	**Location**
Mrs. Katherine Grant	WPQR-TV	Los Angeles, CA
Dr. Manuél Cruz	Miami Herald	Miami, FL
Mr. Richard Logan	Cable News Network	Atlanta, GA
Ms. Barbara Brooks	Associated Press	Chicago, IL

12 pt↓   ↓1X
↓1X

Our initial plans are for the team to spend at least one full day in each of these countries. That, of course, could change. Many different events have been planned. I will be organizing and facilitating meeting with the news programming

B. MULTIPAGE BUSINESS LETTER

(page 2; with page number; multiline list; company name; and enclosure, delivery, copy, postscript, and blind copy notations)

2 **Page number**

staff of one or two of the major networks, touring their facilities, viewing recent broadcasts, and, in general, getting a firsthand view of actual news operations.

Our tentative itinerary calls for a departure date of Monday, July 26. Our arrival city is London. We will spend at least two days there to be sure that all meeting participants have arrived safely.

We should arrive at Heathrow Airport at 7:10 a.m. on Tuesday, July 27. We will immediately go to our hotel and begin our tours the next morning. Would it be possible for us to do the following:
↓2X
Multiline list 1. Meet with various members of your staff sometime on July 28. We would be available from 8:30 a.m. until 1:30 p.m.
2. Receive a copy of your programming log for the week of July 26-30 and especially a minute-by-minute listing of the programming segments for your national news reporting.
↓2X
I would appreciate your contacting Barbara Jones, our liaison, at 202.555.3943 to let us know whether we may study your operations on July 28.
↓2X
Sincerely,
↓2X
Company name METRO BROADCASTING COMPANY
↓4X
Denise J. Watterson

Denise J. Watterson
General Manager
↓2X
rcp
Enclosure notation Enclosures: FCC Report, Biographical Sketches
Delivery notation By FedEx
Copy notation c: Barbara Jones, Manuél Cruz
↓2X
Postscript PS: The Federal Communications Commission will reimburse your organization for any expenses associated with our visit.
↓2X
Blind copy notation bc: Public Relations Office, FCC

C. E-MAIL MESSAGE IN MICROSOFT OUTLOOK

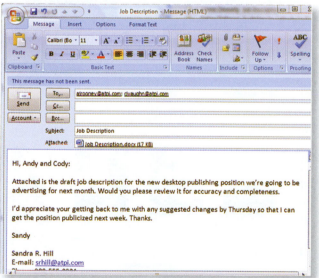

D. E-MAIL MESSAGE IN MSN HOTMAIL

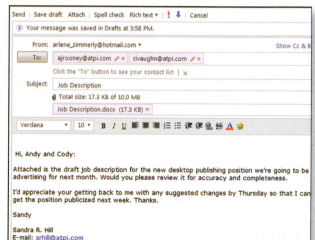

Reference Manual

A. FORMATTING ENVELOPES

A standard large (No. 10) envelope is 9.5 by 4.125 inches. A standard small (No. 6¾) envelope is 6.5 by 3.625 inches.

A window envelope requires no formatting, since the letter is formatted and folded so that the inside address is visible through the window.

Standard large envelope

NATIONAL GEOGRAPHIC SOCIETY
Image Collection & Image Sales
1145 17th Street, NW
Washington, DC 20036-4688, USA

Ms Joan R Hunter
Bolwater Associates
One Parklands Drive
Darien CT 06820-3214

Standard small envelope

Roger J. Michaelson
901 East Benson, Apt. 3
Fort Lauderdale, FL 33301

Mr. Joseph G. Jenshak
17032 Stewart Avenue
Augusta, GA 30904

NATIONAL GEOGRAPHIC SOCIETY
Image Collection & Image Sales
1145 17th Street, NW
Washington, DC 20036-4688, USA

Ms. Renalda Guerrero
BBL Resources
52A Northern Ridge
Fayetteville, PA 17222

Standard window envelope

B. FOLDING LETTERS

To fold a letter for a large envelope:

1. Place the letter *face up,* and fold up the bottom third.
2. Fold the top third down to 0.5 inch from the bottom edge.
3. Insert the last crease into the envelope first, with the flap facing up.

To fold a letter for a small envelope:

1. Place the letter *face up,* and fold up the bottom half to 0.5 inch from the top.
2. Fold the right third over to the left.
3. Fold the left third over to 0.5 inch from the right edge.
4. Insert the last crease into the envelope first, with the flap facing up.

To fold a letter for a window envelope:

1. Place the letter *face down* with the letterhead at the top, and fold the bottom third of the letter up.
2. Fold the top third down so that the address shows.
3. Insert the letter into the envelope so that the address shows through the window.

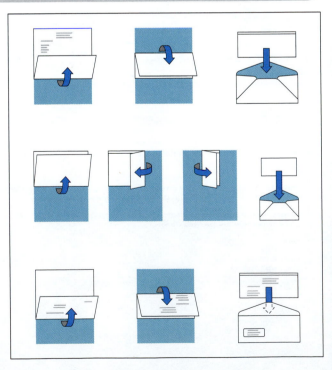

Reference Manual

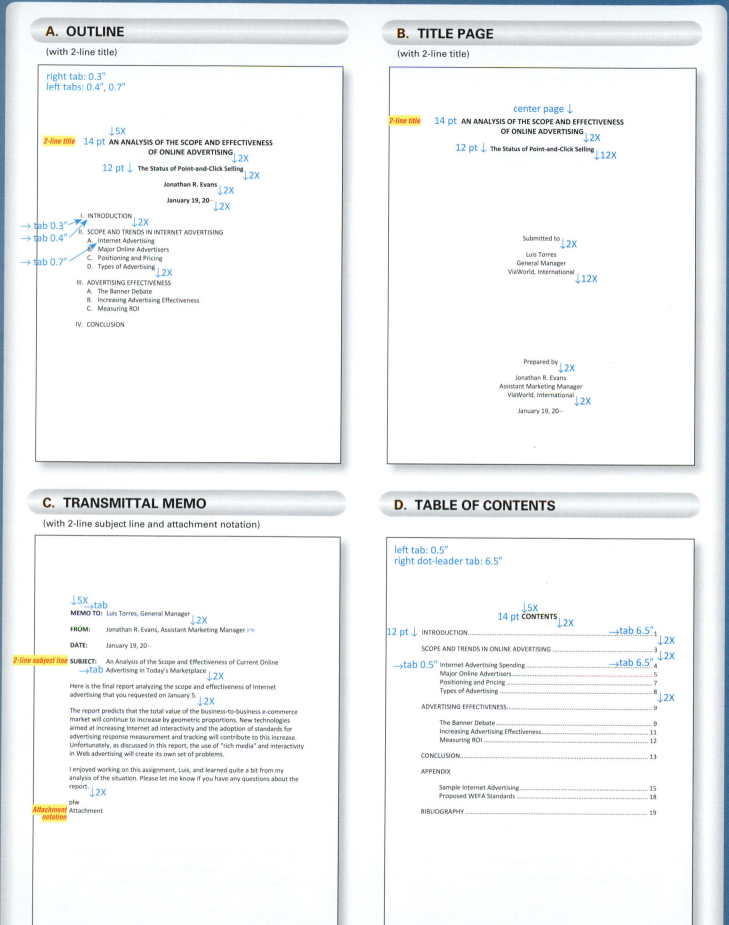

A. OUTLINE
(with 2-line title)

right tab: 0.3"
left tabs: 0.4", 0.7"

↓5X
2-line title 14 pt **AN ANALYSIS OF THE SCOPE AND EFFECTIVENESS OF ONLINE ADVERTISING** ↓2X
12 pt ↓ **The Status of Point-and-Click Selling** ↓2X
Jonathan R. Evans ↓2X
January 19, 20– ↓2X

I. INTRODUCTION ↓2X
→ tab 0.3"
→ tab 0.4" II. SCOPE AND TRENDS IN INTERNET ADVERTISING
   A. Internet Advertising
   B. Major Online Advertisers
→ tab 0.7"   C. Positioning and Pricing
   D. Types of Advertising ↓2X
III. ADVERTISING EFFECTIVENESS
   A. The Banner Debate
   B. Increasing Advertising Effectiveness
   C. Measuring ROI

IV. CONCLUSION

B. TITLE PAGE
(with 2-line title)

center page ↓
2-line title 14 pt **AN ANALYSIS OF THE SCOPE AND EFFECTIVENESS OF ONLINE ADVERTISING** ↓2X
12 pt ↓ **The Status of Point-and-Click Selling** ↓12X

Submitted to ↓2X

Luis Torres
General Manager
ViaWorld, International ↓12X

Prepared by ↓2X
Jonathan R. Evans
Assistant Marketing Manager
ViaWorld, International ↓2X

January 19, 20–

C. TRANSMITTAL MEMO
(with 2-line subject line and attachment notation)

↓5X →tab
MEMO TO: Luis Torres, General Manager ↓2X
FROM: Jonathan R. Evans, Assistant Marketing Manager *jre*
DATE: January 19, 20–
2-line subject line **SUBJECT:** An Analysis of the Scope and Effectiveness of Current Online
→tab Advertising in Today's Marketplace ↓2X

Here is the final report analyzing the scope and effectiveness of Internet advertising that you requested on January 5. ↓2X

The report predicts that the total value of the business-to-business e-commerce market will continue to increase by geometric proportions. New technologies aimed at increasing Internet ad interactivity and the adoption of standards for advertising response measurement and tracking will contribute to this increase. Unfortunately, as discussed in this report, the use of "rich media" and interactivity in Web advertising will create its own set of problems.

I enjoyed working on this assignment, Luis, and learned quite a bit from my analysis of the situation. Please let me know if you have any questions about the report. ↓2X

plw
Attachment notation Attachment

D. TABLE OF CONTENTS

left tab: 0.5"
right dot-leader tab: 6.5"

↓5X
14 pt **CONTENTS** ↓2X

Reference Manual

A. MULTIPAGE BUSINESS REPORT

(page 1; with side and paragraph headings, multiline list, footnote references, and footnotes)

B. MULTIPAGE BUSINESS REPORT

(last page; with page number, indented display, side heading, boxed table with table number and note, and footnote)

C. MULTIPAGE ACADEMIC REPORT

(page 1; with 2-line title, endnote references, and multiline list)

D. MULTIPAGE ACADEMIC REPORT

(last page; with page number, indented display, and endnotes)

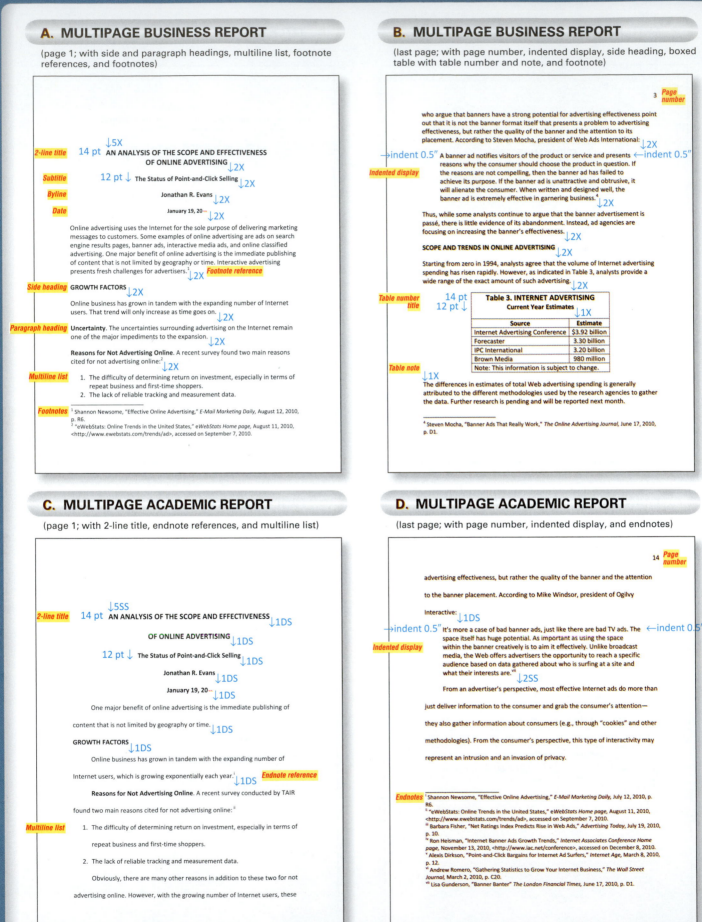

Reference Manual

A. LEFT-BOUND BUSINESS REPORT

(page 1; with 2-line title, single-line list, and footnotes)

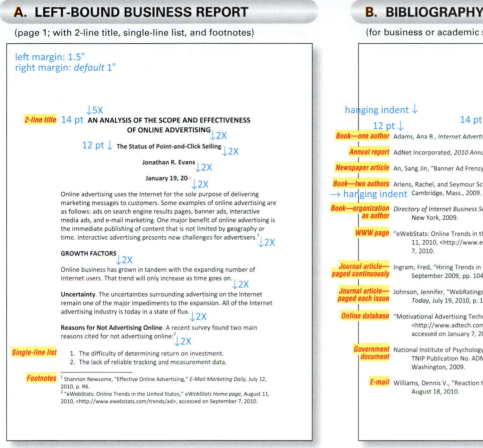

B. BIBLIOGRAPHY

(for business or academic style using either endnotes or footnotes)

C. MEMO REPORT

(page 1, with 2-line subject line, endnote references, and single-line list)

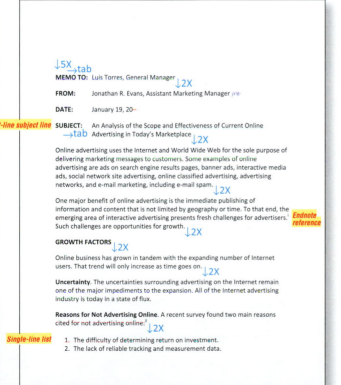

D. FORMATTING REPORTS

Margins, Spacing, and Indents. Begin the first page of each section (for example, the table of contents, first page of the body, and bibliography pages) 2 inches from the top of the page. Begin other pages 1 inch from the top. Use 1-inch default side and bottom margins for all pages. For a left-bound report, add 0.5 inch to the left margin. Single-space business reports. Double-space academic reports and indent paragraphs.

Titles and Headings. Center the title in 14-pt. font. Single-space multiline titles in a single-spaced report, and double-space multiline titles in a double-spaced report. Insert 1 blank line before and after all parts of a heading block (may include the title, subtitle, author, and/or date), and format all lines in bold. Format side headings in bold, at the left margin, with 1 blank line before and after them. Format paragraph headings at the left margin for single-spaced reports and indented for double-spaced reports in bold, followed by a period in bold and one space.

Citations. Format citations using Word's footnote (or endnote) feature.

Margins, Spacing, Headings, and Citations for APA- or MLA-Style Reports. See page R-10.

Reference Manual

A. REPORT IN APA STYLE

(page 3; with header, 2-line title, byline, main heading, subheading, and citations)

top, bottom, and side margins: *default* (1")
double-space throughout

Online Advertising 3 `Header`

`2-line title` — An Analysis of the Scope and Effectiveness
of Online Advertising

`Byline` — Jonathan R. Evans

→ tab Online advertising uses the Internet for the sole purpose of delivering marketing messages to customers. Some examples of online advertising are ads on search engine results pages, banner ads, interactive media ads, online classifieds, advertising networks, and e-mail marketing (Gunderson, 2011, p. D1). `Citation`

One major benefit of online advertising is the immediate publishing of content that is not limited by geography or time. To that end, interactive advertising presents fresh challenges for advertisers (Newsome, 2010).

`Main heading` — Growth Factors

Online business has grown in tandem with the expanding number of Internet users. That trend will only increase as time goes on (Arlens & Schell).

`Subheading` *Uncertainty* ← *Italic*

The uncertainties surrounding Internet advertising are impeding its expansion. A recent survey found two main reasons cited for not advertising online. The first is the difficulty of determining return on investment, especially in terms of repeat business and first-time shoppers. The second is the lack of reliable tracking and measurement data ("eWebStats," 2010).

B. REFERENCES IN APA STYLE

(page 14; with header)

top, bottom, and side margins: *default* (1")
double-space throughout

Online Advertising 14 `Header`

hanging indent ↓ References

`Book—one author` Adams, A. B. (2009). *Internet advertising and the upcoming electronic upheaval.*

→ hanging indent Boston: Brunswick Press.

`Annual report` AdNet Incoporated. (2010). *2010 annual report.* San Francisco: BCI, Inc.

`Newspaper article` An, S. J. (2010, July 12). Banner ad frenzy. *The Wall Street Journal,* p. R6.

`Book—two authors` Arlens, R., & Seymour, S. (2010). *E-vertising.* Cambridge, MA: New England Publishing.

`Book—organization as author` *Directory of business and financial services.* (2009). New York: International Corporate Libraries Association.

`WWW page` eWebStats: Advertising revenues and trends. (n.d.). New York: eMarketer. Retrieved August 11, 2010, from http://www.emarketer.com/ewebstats/2507manu.ad

`Journal article—paged continuously` Ingram, F. (2009). Trends in online advertising. *Personnel Quarterly, 20,* 804-816.

`Journal article—paged each issue` Johnson, J. (2010, July 19). WebRatings Index shows 4% rise in Web ads. *Advertising Today, 39,* 18.

`Online database` *Motivational advertising techniques.* (2010, January). *Advertising Encyclopedia.* Retrieved January 7, 2010, from http://www.adtech.com/ads.html

`Government document` National Institute of Psychology (2009). *Who clicks? An analysis of Internet advertising* (TNIP Publication No. ADM 82-1195). Washington, DC.

C. REPORT IN MLA STYLE

(page 1; with header, heading, 2-line title, and citations)

top, bottom, and side margins: *default* (1")
double-space throughout

Evans 1 `Header`

`Heading` — Jonathan R. Evans
Professor Inman
Management 302
19 January 20—

`2-line title` — An Analysis of the Scope and Effectiveness
of Online Advertising

→ tab Online advertising uses the Internet for the sole purpose of delivering marketing messages to customers. Some examples of online advertising are ads on search engine results pages, banner ads, interactive media ads, social network site advertising, online classifieds, and e-mail marketing (Gunderson D1). `Citation`

One major benefit of online advertising is the immediate publishing of information and content that is not limited by geography or time. To that end, interactive advertising presents fresh challenges for advertisers (Newsome 59).

Online business has grown in tandem with the expanding number of Internet users. That trend will only increase as time goes on (Arlens & Schell 376-379). The uncertainties surrounding Internet advertising remain one of the major impediments to the expansion. A recent survey found two main reasons cited for not advertising online. The first is the difficulty of determining return on investment. The second is the lack of reliable tracking and measurement data.

D. WORKS CITED IN MLA STYLE

(page 14; with header and hanging indent)

top, bottom, and side margins: *default* (1")
double-space throughout

Evans 14 `Header`

hanging indent ↓ Works Cited

`Book—one author` Adams, Ana. B. *Internet Advertising and the Upcoming Electronic Upheaval.*

→ hanging indent Boston: Brunswick Press, 2009.

`Annual report` AdNet Incoporated. *2010 Annual Report.* San Francisco: BCI, Inc., 2010.

`Newspaper article` An, Sang Jin. "Banner Ad Frenzy." *The Wall Street Journal,* 12 July 2010: R6.

`Book—two authors` Arlens, Rachel, and Seymour Schell. *E-vertising.* Cambridge, MA: New England Publishing, 2009.

`Book—organization as author` Corporate Libraries Association. *Directory of Business and Financial Services.* New York: Corporate Libraries Association, 2009.

`WWW page` "eWebStats: Advertising Revenues and Trends." 11 Aug. 2009. 7 Jan. 2010 <http://www.emarketer.com/ewebstats/ad>.

`Journal article—paged continuously` Ingram, Frank. "Trends in Online Advertising." *Personnel Quarterly* 20 (2010): 804-816.

`Journal article—paged each issue` Johnson, June. "WRI shows 4% rise in Web ads." *WebAds Today* 19 July 2010: 18.

`Online database` *Motivational Advertising Techniques.* 2010. Advertising Encyclopedia. 7 Jan. 2010 <http://www.adtech.com/ads.html>.

`Government document` National Institute of Psychology. *Who clicks?* TNIP Publication No. ADM 82-1195. Washington, DC. GPO: 2010.

`E-mail` Williams, Dan V. "Reaction to Internet Ads." E-mail to the author. 18 Aug. 2010.

Reference Manual

A. MEETING AGENDA

↓5X
14 pt MILES HARDWARE EXECUTIVE COMMITTEE ↓2X
12 pt ↓ Meeting Agenda ↓2X
June 7, 20— ↓2X

Numbered list: default format
1. Call to order
2. Approval of minutes of May 5 meeting
3. Progress report on building addition and parking lot restrictions (Norman Hodges and Anthony Pascarelli)
4. May 15 draft of Five-Year Plan
5. Review of National Hardware Association annual convention
6. Employee grievance filed by Ellen Burrows (John Landstrom)
7. New expense-report forms (Anne Richards)
8. Announcements
9. Adjournment

B. MINUTES OF A MEETING

↓5X
14 pt RESOURCE COMMITTEE ↓2X
12 pt ↓ Minutes of the Meeting ↓2X
March 13, 20— ↓1X

ATTENDANCE	The Resource Committee met on March 13, 20—, at the Airport Sheraton in Portland, Oregon, with all members present. Michael Davis, chairperson, called the meeting to order at 2:30 p.m. ↓1X
APPROVAL OF MINUTES	The minutes of the January 27 meeting were read and approved as presented.
OLD BUSINESS	The members of the committee reviewed the sales brochure on electronic copyboards and agreed to purchase one for the conference room. Cynthia Giovanni will secure quotations from at least two suppliers.
NEW BUSINESS	The committee reviewed a request from the Purchasing Department for three new computers. After extensive discussion regarding the appropriate use of the computers and software to be purchased, the committee approved the request.
ADJOURNMENT	The meeting was adjourned at 4:45 p.m. The next meeting is scheduled for April 13 in Suite B. ↓2X Respectfully submitted, ↓4X *D. S. Madsen* D. S. Madsen, Secretary

(Note: Table shown with "View Gridlines" active.)

C. ITINERARY

↓5X
14 pt PORTLAND SALES MEETING ↓2X
12 pt ↓ Itinerary for Dorothy Turner ↓2X
March 12-15, 20— ↓1X

THURSDAY, MARCH 12 ↓1X	
5:10 p.m.-7:06 p.m.	Flight from Detroit to Portland; Northwest 83 (800-555-1212); e-ticket; Seat 8D; nonstop. ↓2X Jack Weatherford (Home: 503-555-8029; Office: 503-555-7631) will meet your flight on Thursday, provide transportation during your visit, and return you to the airport on Saturday morning. ↓2X Airport Sheraton (503-555-4032) King-sized bed, nonsmoking room; late arrival guaranteed; Reservation No. 30ZM6-02. ↓1X
FRIDAY, MARCH 13	
9 a.m.-5:30 p.m.	Portland Sales Meeting 1931 Executive Way, Suite 10 Portland, OR 97211 (503-555-7631)
SATURDAY, MARCH 14	
7:30 a.m.-2:47 p.m.	Flight from Portland to Detroit; Northwest 360; e-ticket; Seat 9a; nonstop.

(Note: Table shown with "View Gridlines" active.)

D. LEGAL DOCUMENT

(with line numbers)

left tabs: 1", 3.25"
right tab: 6.5"

line numbers (court documents only)

```
1   STATE OF NEVADA              → tab 6.5" IN DISTRICT COURT ↓2X
2
3   COUNTY OF CLARK                   NORTHEAST JUDICIAL DISTRICT ↓2X
4
5   JOHN C. SMITH       → tab 3.25"  →    NO.   1 space, 20 underscores
6   209 East Clark Avenue            ) tab 6.5"
7   Las Vegas, NV 89155-1603         )
8                                    )
9   → tab 1" Plaintiff,  → tab 3.25")
10                                   )
11            vs.                    )      → tab 6.5" SUMMONS
12                                   )
13  FAITH GEORGIA                    )
14                                   )
15          Defendant.               )
16                                   ) ↓2X
17  THE STATE OF NEVADA TO THE ABOVE-NAMED DEFENDANT: ↓2X
18
19  → tab 1" You are hereby summoned and required to appear and defend
20  against the Complaint in this action, which is hereby served upon you by serving
21  upon the undersigned an Answer or other proper response within twenty (20)
22  days after the service of the Summons and Complaint upon you, exclusive of the
23  day of service. ↓2X
24
25          If you fail to do so, judgment by default will be taken against you for
26  the relief demanded in the Complaint.
27
28          SIGNED this _____ day of July, 20—. ↓2X
29  1 space;                         underscores to the right margin
30  5 underscores;
31  1 space            → tab 3.25" Jim Roe → tab 6.5" Attorney at Law
32                                   229 South Civic Way
33                                   Laughlin, NV 89029-2648
34                                   Telephone: 702-555-1205
35                                   Attorney for Plaintiff
```

A. RESUME

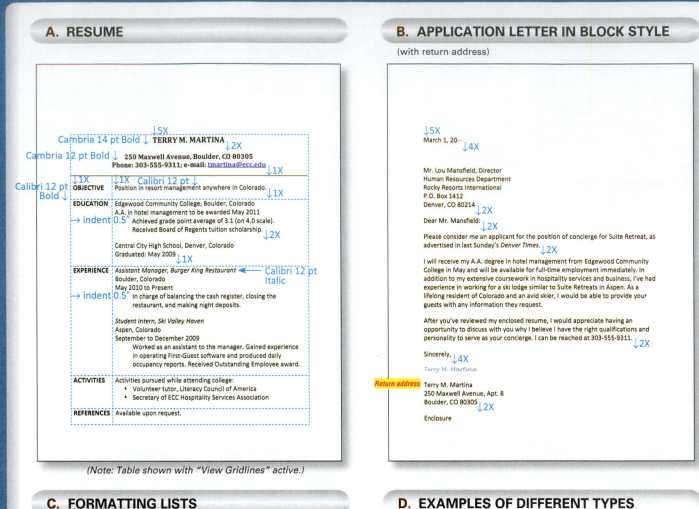

(Note: Table shown with "View Gridlines" active.)

B. APPLICATION LETTER IN BLOCK STYLE

(with return address)

↓5X
March 1, 20--
↓4X

Mr. Lou Mansfield, Director
Human Resources Department
Rocky Resorts International
P.O. Box 1412
Denver, CO 80214
↓2X

Dear Mr. Mansfield:
↓2X

Please consider me an applicant for the position of concierge for Suite Retreat, as advertised in last Sunday's *Denver Times.*
↓2X

I will receive my A.A. degree in hotel management from Edgewood Community College in May and will be available for full-time employment immediately. In addition to my extensive coursework in hospitality services and business, I've had experience in working for a ski lodge similar to Suite Retreats in Aspen. As a lifelong resident of Colorado and an avid skier, I would be able to provide your guests with any information they request.

After you've reviewed my enclosed resume, I would appreciate having an opportunity to discuss with you why I believe I have the right qualifications and personality to serve as your concierge. I can be reached at 303-555-9311.
↓2X

Sincerely, ↓4X

Terry M. Martina

Return address Terry M. Martina
250 Maxwell Avenue, Apt. 8
Boulder, CO 80305
↓2X

Enclosure

C. FORMATTING LISTS

Numbers or bullets are used in documents to call attention to items in a list and to increase readability. If the sequence of the list items is important, use numbers rather than bullets.

- Insert 1 blank line before and after the list.
- Use Word's default format for all lists in either single- or double-spaced documents, including lists in documents such as a meeting agenda. Any carryover lines will be indented automatically.
- Use the same line spacing (single or double) between lines in the list as is used in the rest of the document.

The three bulleted and numbered lists shown at the right are all formatted correctly.

D. EXAMPLES OF DIFFERENT TYPES OF LISTS

According to the Internet Advertising Bureau, the following are the most common types of advertising on the Internet:

- Banner ads that feature some type of appropriate animation to attract the viewer's attention and interest.
- Sponsorship, in which an advertiser sponsors a content-based Web site.
- Interstitials, ads that flash up while a page downloads.

There is now considerable controversy about the effectiveness of banner advertising. As previously noted, a central goal of banner advertisements is to

*****

According to the Internet Advertising Bureau, the following are the most common types of advertising on the Internet, shown in order of popularity:

1. Banner ads
2. Sponsorship
3. Interstitials

There is now considerable controversy about the effectiveness of banner advertising. As previously noted, a central goal of banner advertisements is to

*****

According to the Internet Advertising Bureau, the following are the most common types of advertising on the Internet:

- Banner ads that feature some type of appropriate animation to attract the viewer's attention and interest.

- Sponsorship, in which an advertiser sponsors a Web site.

- Interstitials, ads that flash up while a page downloads.

There is now considerable controversy about the effectiveness of banner advertising. As previously noted, a central goal of banner advertisements is to

Reference Manual

A. BOXED TABLE

(with subtitle; bottom-aligned and braced column headings; left- and right-aligned columns; total line and table note)

B. OPEN TABLE

(with 2-line title; 2-line centered, bottom-aligned column headings; left- and right-aligned columns; column entries with dollar and percent signs)

(Note: Table shown with "View Gridlines" active.)

C. RULED TABLE

(with table number, title, centered column headings, and total line)

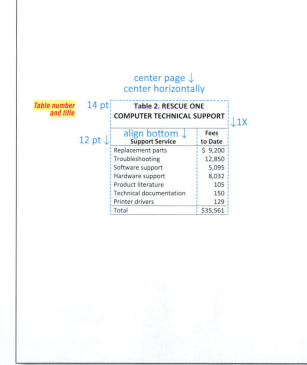

(Note: Table shown with "View Gridlines" active.)

D. FORMATTING TABLES

The three basic styles of tables are boxed, open, and ruled. Tables have vertical columns (Column A), horizontal rows (Row 1), and intersecting cells (Cell A1). Center a table vertically that appears alone on the page. Insert 1 blank line before and after a table that appears within a document. Automatically adjust column widths and horizontally center all tables.

Heading Block. Merge any cells in Row 1, and type the heading block. Center and bold throughout. Type the title in all-caps, 14-pt. font, and the subtitle in upper- and lowercase, 12-pt. font. If a table has a number, type *Table* in upper- and lowercase. Follow the table number with a period and 1 space. Insert 1 blank line below the heading block.

Column Headings. Center column headings. Type in upper- and lowercase and bold. Bottom-align all column headings if a row includes a 2-line column heading. Merge desired cells for braced headings.

Column Entries. Left-align text columns, and right-align number columns. Capitalize only the first word and proper nouns in column entries.

Column Entry Dollar and Percent Signs. Insert the dollar sign only before the amount in the first entry and before a total amount entry. Align the dollar sign with the longest amount in the column, inserting spaces after the dollar sign as needed (allowing for 2 spaces for each digit and 1 space for each comma). Repeat the percent sign for each number in each column entry (unless the column heading identifies the data as percentages).

Table Note and Total Line. For a note line, merge the cells of the last row and use "Note" followed by a colon. For a total line, add a top and bottom border, use "Total" or "Totals" as appropriate, and add a percent or dollar sign if needed.

Reference Manual

A. FORMATTING BUSINESS FORMS

Many business forms can be created and filled in by using templates that are provided within commercial word processing software. Template forms can be used "as is" or they can be edited. Templates can also be used to create customized forms for any business.

When a template is opened, the form is displayed on screen. The user can then fill in the necessary information, including personalized company information. Data are entered into cells or fields, and you can move quickly from field to field with a single keystroke—usually by pressing TAB or ENTER.

Masco Shipping   **PURCHASE ORDER**

1335 Dublin Road
Columbus, OH 43215
Phone 614-555-3971 Fax 614-555-3980

The following number must appear on all related
correspondence, shipping papers, and invoices:
P.O. NUMBER: 1074

TO: SHIP TO:
Reliable Office Supply
Great Lakes Distribution Center
1001 West Van Buren Street
Chicago, IL 60607

P.O. DATE	REQUISITIONER	SHIPPED VIA	F.O.B. POINT	TERMS
10/22/--	DV	Fed Ex		

QTY	UNIT	DESCRIPTION	UNIT PRICE	TOTAL
120	HO2048	Perforated ruled pads	$ 0.48	$ 57.60
36	564LQ4	Recyclable storage boxes, legal size	3.69	132.84
2	22Z398	Paper punch	58.67	117.34
1	B48560	Hi-style tackboard, 24" x 36", burgundy frame, blue fabric	31.98	31.98
1	J22502	Kraft catalog envelopes, 10" x 13", clasp with gummed flap, box of 500	104.86	104.86
		SUBTOTAL		444.62
		SALES TAX		26.77
		SHIPPING & HANDLING		
		OTHER		
		TOTAL		$471.39

1. Please send two copies of your invoice.
2. Enter this order in accordance with the prices, terms, delivery method, and specifications listed above.
3. Please notify us immediately if you are unable to ship as specified.
4. Send all correspondence to:
   Masco Shipping Lines
   1335 Dublin Road
   Columbus, OH 43215
   Phone 614-555-3971 Fax 614-555-3980

Authorized by   Date

B. U.S. POSTAL SERVICE ABBREVIATIONS

(for States, Territories, and Canadian Provinces)

States and Territories

Alabama	AL
Alaska	AK
Arizona	AZ
Arkansas	AR
California	CA
Colorado	CO
Connecticut	CT
Delaware	DE
District of Columbia	DC
Florida	FL
Georgia	GA
Guam	GU
Hawaii	HI
Idaho	ID
Illinois	IL
Indiana	IN
Iowa	IA
Kansas	KS
Kentucky	KY
Louisiana	LA
Maine	ME
Maryland	MD
Massachusetts	MA
Michigan	MI
Minnesota	MN
Mississippi	MS
Missouri	MO
Montana	MT
Nebraska	NE
Nevada	NV
New Hampshire	NH
New Jersey	NJ
New Mexico	NM
New York	NY
North Carolina	NC
North Dakota	ND
Ohio	OH
Oklahoma	OK
Oregon	OR
Pennsylvania	PA
Puerto Rico	PR
Rhode Island	RI
South Carolina	SC
South Dakota	SD
Tennessee	TN
Texas	TX
Utah	UT
Vermont	VT
Virgin Islands	VI
Virginia	VA
Washington	WA
West Virginia	WV
Wisconsin	WI
Wyoming	WY

Canadian Provinces

Alberta	AB
British Columbia	BC
Labrador	LB
Manitoba	MB
New Brunswick	NB
Newfoundland	NF
Northwest Territories	NT
Nova Scotia	NS
Ontario	ON
Prince Edward Island	PE
Quebec	PQ
Saskatchewan	SK
Yukon Territory	YT

C. PROOFREADERS' MARKS

Proofreaders' Marks		Draft	Final Copy
⌒	Omit space	data base	database
v or ∧	Insert	if hes going	if he's not going,
≡	Capitalize	Maple street	Maple Street
ℓ	Delete	a final draft	a draft
#	Insert space	allready to	all ready to
when/if	Change word	and if you	and when you
/	Use lowercase letter	our President	our president
¶	Paragraph	… to use it. We can	… to use it. We can
•••	Don't delete	a true story	a true story
O	Spell out	the only 1	the only one
∽	Transpose	they all see	they see all

Proofreaders' Marks		Draft	Final Copy
SS	Single-space	first line / second line	first line / second line
ds	Double-space	first line / second line	first line / second line
⌐	Move right	Please send	Please send
⌐	Move left	May I	May I
∿	Bold	Column Heading	**Column Heading**
ital	Italic	Time magazine	*Time* magazine
u/l	Underline	Time magazine	Time magazine readers
♂	Move as shown	readers will see	will see

Language Arts For Business

(50 "must-know" rules)

PUNCTUATION

Commas

RULE 1
, direct address
(L. 21)

Use commas before and after a name used in direct address.

Thank you, John, for responding to my e-mail so quickly.
Ladies and gentlemen, the program has been canceled.

RULE 2
, independent clause
(L. 27)

Use a comma between independent clauses joined by a coordinate conjunction (unless both clauses are short).

Ellen left her job with IBM, and she and her sister went to Paris.
But: Ellen left her job with IBM and went to Paris with her sister.
But: John drove and I navigated.

Note: An independent clause is one that can stand alone as a complete sentence. The most common coordinate conjunctions are *and*, *but*, *or*, and *nor*.

The under-line calls attention to a point in the sentence where a comma might mis-takenly be inserted.

RULE 3
, introductory expression
(L. 27)

Use a comma after an introductory expression (unless it is a short prepositional phrase).

Before we can make a decision, we must have all the facts.
But: In 2004 our nation elected a new president.

Note: An introductory expression is a group of words that come before the subject and verb of the independent clause. Common prepositions are *to*, *in*, *on*, *of*, *at*, *by*, *for*, and *with*.

RULE 4
, direct quotation
(L. 41)

Use a comma before and after a direct quotation.

James said, "I shall return," and then left.

RULE 5
, date
(L. 51)

Use a comma before and after the year in a complete date.

We will arrive on June 2, 2006, for the conference.
But: We will arrive on June 2 for the conference.

RULE 6
, place
(L. 51)

Use a comma before and after a state or country that follows a city (but not before a ZIP Code).

Joan moved to Vancouver, British Columbia, in May.
Send the package to Douglasville, GA 30135, by Express Mail.
But: Send the package to Georgia by Express Mail.

RULE 7 , series (L. 61)	**Use a comma between each item in a series of three or more.**

We need to order paper, toner, and font cartridges for the printer.

They saved their work, exited their program, and turned off their computers when they finished.

Note: Do not use a comma after the last item in a series.

RULE 8 , transitional expression (L. 61)	**Use a comma before and after a transitional expression or independent comment.**

It is critical, therefore, that we finish the project on time.

Our present projections, you must admit, are inadequate.

But: You must admit our present projections are inadequate.

Note: Examples of transitional expressions and independent comments are *in addition to, therefore, however, on the other hand, as a matter of fact,* and *unfortunately.*

RULE 9 , nonessential expression (L. 71)	**Use a comma before and after a nonessential expression.**

Andre, who was there, can verify the statement.

But: Anyone who was there can verify the statement.

Van's first book, *Crisis of Management*, was not discussed.

Van's book *Crisis of Management* was not discussed.

Note: A nonessential expression is a group of words that may be omitted without changing the basic meaning of the sentence. Always examine the noun or pronoun that comes before the expression to determine whether the noun needs the expression to complete its meaning. If it does, the expression is *essential* and does *not* take a comma.

RULE 10 , adjacent adjectives (L. 71)	**Use a comma between two adjacent adjectives that modify the same noun.**

We need an intelligent, enthusiastic individual for this job.

But: Please order a new bulletin board for our main conference room.

Note: Do not use a comma after the second adjective. Also, do not use a comma if the first adjective modifies the combined idea of the second adjective and the noun (for example, *bulletin board* and *conference room* in the second example above).

Semicolons

RULE 11 ; no conjunction (L. 97)	**Use a semicolon to separate two closely related independent clauses that are not joined by a conjunction (such as *and, but, or,* or *nor*).**

Management favored the vote; stockholders did not.

But: Management favored the vote, but stockholders did not.

RULE 12 ; series (L. 97)	**Use a semicolon to separate three or more items in a series if any of the items already contain commas.**

Staff meetings were held on Thursday, May 7; Monday, June 7; and Friday, June 12.

Note: Be sure to insert the semicolon *between* (not within) the items in a series.

Reference Manual

Hyphens

RULE 13
- number
(L. 57)

Hyphenate compound numbers between twenty-one and ninety-nine and fractions that are expressed as words.

> Twenty-nine recommendations were approved by at least three-fourths of the members.

RULE 14
- compound adjective
(L. 67)

Hyphenate compound adjectives that come before a noun (unless the first word is an adverb ending in -ly).

> We reviewed an up-to-date report on Wednesday.
> But: The report was up to date.
> But: We reviewed the highly rated report.

Note: A compound adjective is two or more words that function as a unit to describe a noun.

Apostrophes

RULE 15
' singular noun
(L. 37)

Use 's to form the possessive of singular nouns.

> The hurricane's force caused major damage to North Carolina's coastline.

RULE 16
' plural noun
(L. 37)

Use only an apostrophe to form the possessive of plural nouns that end in s.

> The investors' goals were outlined in the stockholders' report.
> But: The investors outlined their goals in the report to the stockholders.
> But: The women's and children's clothing was on sale.

RULE 17
' pronoun
(L. 37)

Use 's to form the possessive of indefinite pronouns (such as someone's or anybody's); do not use an apostrophe with personal pronouns (such as hers, his, its, ours, theirs, and yours).

> She could select anybody's paper for a sample.
> It's time to put the file back into its cabinet.

Colons

RULE 18
: explanatory material
(L. 91)

Use a colon to introduce explanatory material that follows an independent clause.

> The computer satisfies three criteria: speed, cost, and power.
> But: The computer satisfies the three criteria of speed, cost, and power.
> Remember this: only one coupon is allowed per customer.

Note: An independent clause can stand alone as a complete sentence. Do not capitalize the word following the colon.

Periods

RULE 19
. polite request
(L. 91)

Use a period to end a sentence that is a polite request.

> Will you please call me if I can be of further assistance.

Note: Consider a sentence a polite request if you expect the reader to respond by doing as you ask rather than by giving a yes-or-no answer.

Quotation Marks

RULE 20
" direct quotation
(L. 41)

Use quotation marks around a direct quotation.

> Harrison responded by saying, "Their decision does not affect us."
> But: Harrison responded by saying that their decision does not affect us.

RULE 21
" title
(L. 41)

Use quotation marks around the title of a newspaper or magazine article, chapter in a book, report, and similar terms.

> The most helpful article I found was "Multimedia for All."

Italics (or Underline)

RULE 22
title or title
(L. 41)

Italicize (or underline) the titles of books, magazines, newspapers, and other complete published works.

> Grisham's *The Brethren* was reviewed in a recent *USA Today* article.

GRAMMAR

Sentences

RULE 23
fragment
(L. 21)

Avoid sentence fragments.

> Not: She had always wanted to be a financial manager. But had not had the needed education.

> But: She had always wanted to be a financial manager but had not had the needed education.

Note: A fragment is a part of a sentence that is incorrectly punctuated as a complete sentence. In the first example above, "but had not had the needed education" is not a complete sentence because it does not contain a subject.

RULE 24
run-on
(L. 21)

Avoid run-on sentences.

> Not: Mohamed is a competent worker he has even passed the MOS exam.
> Not: Mohamed is a competent worker, he has even passed the MOS exam.
> But: Mohamed is a competent worker; he has even passed the MOS exam.
> Or: Mohamed is a competent worker. He has even passed the MOS exam.

Note: A run-on sentence is two independent clauses that run together without any punctuation between them or with only a comma between them.

Agreement

RULE 25
agreement singular
agreement plural
(L. 67)

Use singular verbs and pronouns with singular subjects; use plural verbs and pronouns with plural subjects.

> I was happy with my performance.
> Janet and Phoenix were happy with their performance.
> Among the items discussed were our raises and benefits.

RULE 26
agreement pronoun
(L. 81)

Some pronouns (*anybody, each, either, everybody, everyone, much, neither, no one, nobody,* and *one*) are always singular and take a singular verb. Other pronouns (*all, any, more, most, none,* and *some*) may be singular or plural, depending on the noun to which they refer.

> Each of the employees has finished his or her task.
> Much remains to be done.
> Most of the pie was eaten, but most of the cookies were left.

RULE 27
agreement intervening words
(L. 81)

Disregard any intervening words that come between the subject and verb when establishing agreement.

> That box, containing the books and pencils, has not been found.
> Alex, accompanied by Tricia and Roxy, is attending the conference and taking his computer.

RULE 28
agreement nearer noun
(L. 101)

If two subjects are joined by *or, either/or, neither/nor,* or *not only/but also,* make the verb agree with the subject nearer to the verb.

> Neither the coach nor the players are at home.
> Not only the coach but also the referee is at home.
> But: Both the coach and the referee are at home.

Reference Manual

Pronouns

RULE 29
nominative pronoun
(L. 107)

Use nominative pronouns (such as *I, he, she, we, they,* and *who*) as subjects of a sentence or clause.

> The programmer and <u>he</u> are reviewing the code.
> Barb is a person <u>who</u> can do the job.

RULE 30
objective pronoun
(L. 107)

Use objective pronouns (such as *me, him, her, us, them,* and *whom*) as objects of a verb, preposition, or infinitive.

> The code was reviewed by the programmer and <u>him</u>.
> Barb is the type of person <u>whom</u> we can trust.

Adjectives and Adverbs

RULE 31
adjective/adverb
(L. 101)

Use comparative adjectives and adverbs (*-er, more,* and *less*) when referring to two nouns or pronouns; use superlative adjectives and adverbs (*-est, most,* and *least*) when referring to more than two.

> The <u>shorter</u> of the <u>two</u> training sessions is the <u>more</u> helpful one.
> The <u>longest</u> of the <u>three</u> training sessions is the <u>least</u> helpful one.

Word Usage

RULE 32
accept/except
(L. 117)

***Accept* means "to agree to"; *except* means "to leave out."**

> All employees <u>except</u> the maintenance staff should <u>accept</u> the agreement.

RULE 33
affect/effect
(L. 117)

***Affect* is most often used as a verb meaning "to influence"; *effect* is most often used as a noun meaning "result."**

> The ruling will <u>affect</u> our domestic operations but will have no <u>effect</u> on our Asian operations.

RULE 34
farther/further
(L. 117)

***Farther* refers to distance; *further* refers to extent or degree.**

> The <u>farther</u> we drove, the <u>further</u> agitated he became.

RULE 35
personal/personnel
(L. 117)

***Personal* means "private"; *personnel* means "employees."**

> All <u>personnel</u> agreed not to use e-mail for <u>personal</u> business.

RULE 36
principal/principle
(L. 117)

***Principal* means "primary"; *principle* means "rule."**

> The <u>principle</u> of fairness is our <u>principal</u> means of dealing with customers.

MECHANICS

Capitalization

RULE 37
≡ sentence
(L. 31)

Capitalize the first word of a sentence.

> Please prepare a summary of your activities.

RULE 38
≡ proper noun
(L. 31)

Capitalize proper nouns and adjectives derived from proper nouns.

> Judy Hendrix drove to Albuquerque in her new Pontiac convertible.

Note: A proper noun is the official name of a particular person, place, or thing.

RULE 39
≡ time
(L. 31)

Capitalize the names of the days of the week, months, holidays, and religious days (but do not capitalize the names of the seasons).

> On Thursday, November 25, we will celebrate Thanksgiving, the most popular holiday in the fall.

RULE 40
≡ noun #
(L. 77)

Capitalize nouns followed by a number or letter (except for the nouns *line, note, page, paragraph,* and *size*).

> Please read Chapter 5, which begins on page 94.

RULE 41
≡ compass point
(L. 77)

Capitalize compass points (such as *north, south,* or *northeast*) only when they designate definite regions.

> From Montana we drove south to reach the Southwest.

RULE 42
≡ organization
(L. 111)

Capitalize common organizational terms (such as *advertising department* and *finance committee*) only when they are the actual names of the units in the writer's own organization and when they are preceded by the word *the*.

> The report from the Advertising Department is due today.
> But: Our advertising department will submit its report today.

RULE 43
≡ course
(L. 111)

Capitalize the names of specific course titles but not the names of subjects or areas of study.

> I have enrolled in Accounting 201 and will also take a marketing course.

Number Expression

RULE 44
general
(L. 47)

In general, spell out numbers zero through ten, and use figures for numbers above ten.

> We rented two movies for tonight.
> The decision was reached after 27 precincts sent in their results.

RULE 45
figure
(L. 47)

Use figures for
- **Dates. (Use *st, d,* or *th* only if the day comes before the month.)**
  The tax report is due on April 15 (not *April 15th*).
  We will drive to the camp on the 23d (or *23rd* or *23ʳᵈ*) of May.
- **All numbers if two or more *related* numbers both above and below ten are used in the same sentence.**
  Mr. Carter sent in 7 receipts, and Ms. Cantrell sent in 22.
  But: The 13 accountants owned three computers each.
- **Measurements (time, money, distance, weight, and percent).**
  The $500 statue we delivered at 7 a.m. weighed 6 pounds.
- **Mixed numbers.**
  Our sales are up 9½ (or *9.5*) percent over last year.

RULE 46
word
(L. 57)

Spell out
- **A number used as the first word of a sentence.**
  Seventy-five people attended the conference in San Diego.
- **The shorter of two adjacent numbers.**
  We have ordered 3 two-pound cakes and one 5-pound cake for the reception.
- **The words *million* and *billion* in round numbers (do not use decimals with round numbers).**
  Not: A $5.00 ticket can win $28,000,000 in this month's lottery.
  But: A $5 ticket can win $28 million in this month's lottery.
- **Fractions.**
  Almost one-half of the audience responded to the question.

Abbreviations

RULE 47
abbreviate none
(L. 67)

In general business writing, do not abbreviate common words (such as *dept.* or *pkg.*), compass points, units of measure, or the names of months, days of the week, cities, or states (except in addresses).
  Almost one-half of the audience indicated they were at least 5 <u>feet</u> 8 inches tall.
Note: Do not insert a comma between the parts of a single measurement.

RULE 48
abbreviate measure
(L. 87)

In technical writing, on forms, and in tables, abbreviate units of measure when they occur frequently. Do not use periods.
  14 oz   5 ft 10 in   50 mph   2 yrs 10 mo

RULE 49
abbreviate lowercase
(L. 87)

In most lowercase abbreviations made up of single initials, use a period after each initial but no internal spaces.
  a.m.   p.m.   i.e.   e.g.   e.o.m.
  Exceptions: mph   mpg   wpm

RULE 50
abbreviate ≡
(L. 87)

In most all-capital abbreviations made up of single initials, do not use periods or internal spaces.
  OSHA   PBS   NBEA   WWW   VCR   MBA
  Exceptions: U.S.A.   A.A.   B.S.   Ph.D.   P.O.   B.C.   A.D.

The Alphabet, Number, and Symbol Keys

Keyboarding in Arts, Audio, Video Technology, and Communication Services

Occupations in this cluster deal with organizing and communicating information to the public in various forms and media.

This cluster includes jobs in radio and television broadcasting, journalism, motion pictures, the recording industry, the performing arts, multimedia publishing, and the entertainment services. Book editors, computer artists, technical writers, radio announcers, news correspondents, camera operators, and home page designers are just a few jobs within this cluster.

Qualifications and Skills

Strong oral and written communication skills and technical skills are necessary for anyone in communications and media. Without a doubt, competent keyboarding skill is extremely advantageous.

Working in the media requires creativity, talent, and accurate use of language. In journalism, being observant, thinking clearly, and seeing the significance of events are all of utmost importance. Announcers must have exceptional voices, excellent speaking skills, and a unique style. The ability to work under pressure is important in all areas of media.

Goals

Keyboarding

- Type by touch the letter, number, and symbol keys.
- Demonstrate proper typing technique.
- Use the correct spacing with punctuation.
- Type at least 28 words per minute on a 2-minute timed writing with no more than 5 errors.

Objective Test

- Answer questions with acceptable accuracy on an objective test.

Keyboarding: The Alphabet

LESSON 1

Home-Row Keys: A S D F J K L ;
SPACE BAR ENTER BACKSPACE

LESSON 2

New Keys: E N T

LESSON 3

New Keys: O R H

LESSON 4

New Keys: I LEFT SHIFT .

LESSON 5

New Keys: B U C

Home-Row Keys

Goals

- Touch-type the home-row keys—A S D F J K L ;.
- Touch-type the Space Bar, Enter, and Backspace keys.
- Type at least 10wpm/1'/3e; that is, type at least 10 words per minute (wpm) on a 1-minute timed writing while making no more than 3 uncorrected errors.

New Keys

A. HOME-ROW POSITION

The A S D F J K L and ; keys are called the *home-row keys.*

1. Place the fingers of your left hand lightly over the A, S, D, and F keys and the fingers of your right hand lightly over the J, K, L, and ; keys, as shown in the illustration below.
2. Feel the raised markers on the F and J keys; they will help you keep your fingers on the home-row keys. You are now in home-row position. Each finger is named for the home-row key it controls. Thus, your left little finger is known as the A finger, and your right little finger is known as the Sem finger (short for *semicolon*).

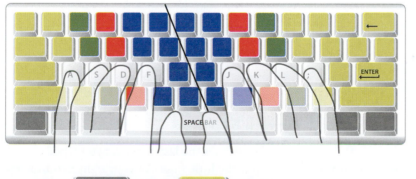

B. THE  SPACE BAR AND ENTER KEYS

The Space Bar is located beneath the letter keys and is used to space between words and after punctuation marks. Tap the Space Bar with a downward and inward (toward your body) motion of the right thumb.

The ENTER key moves the insertion point to the beginning of a new line. Reach to the ENTER key with the Sem finger (the little finger of your right hand), keeping your J finger at home. Quickly return the Sem finger to home-row position after tapping ENTER.

C. PRACTICE THE HOME-ROW KEYS

Type each line 1 time, pressing the SPACE BAR where you see a space and pressing the ENTER key at the end of each line (indicated by ↵). Tap ENTER 2 times (indicated by ↵ ↵) to insert a blank line between each set of drill lines.

```
1  asdf jkl; asdf jkl; asdf jkl; ↵
2  asdf jkl; asdf jkl; asdf jkl; ↵↵

3  asdf jkl; asdf jkl; asdf jkl; ↵
4  asdf jkl; asdf jkl; asdf jkl; ↵
```

Say the name of each key to yourself as you type it.

D. THE F AND J KEYS

```
5  fff fff jjj jjj fff jjj fjf fjf jfj jfj fff fj jf
6  fff fff jjj jjj fff jjj fjf fjf jfj jfj fff fj jf
```

E. THE D AND K KEYS

```
7  ddd ddd kkk kkk ddd kkk dkd dkd kdk kdk ddd dk kd
8  ddd ddd kkk kkk ddd kkk dkd dkd kdk kdk ddd dk kd
```

Rest your other fingers *lightly* over the keys while you're typing.

F. THE S AND L KEYS

```
9   sss lll sss lll sss lll sls sls lsl lsl sss sl ls
10  sss lll sss lll sss lll sls sls lsl lsl sss sl ls
```

G. THE A AND ; KEYS

```
11  aaa ;;; aaa ;;; aaa ;;; a;a a;a ;a; ;a; aaa a; ;a
12  aaa ;;; aaa ;;; aaa ;;; a;a a;a ;a; ;a; aaa a; ;a
```

Use the Sem finger.

H. THE ← KEY

The BACKSPACE key deletes the last character you typed. Reach to the BACKSPACE key with the Sem finger (the little finger of your right hand), keeping your J finger at home. Quickly return the Sem finger to home-row position after tapping BACKSPACE.

Looking at your keyboard and keeping your J finger at home, reach for and quickly press the BACKSPACE key and immediately return your little finger to the Sem key. Do this several times—until you can make the reach without looking at your fingers.

In the drill line below, follow these directions:

1. Type the group of letters as shown.
2. When you reach the BACKSPACE sign (←), backspace 1 time to delete the last keystroke typed.
3. Then type the next letter. For example, you will type *as*, press BACKSPACE 1 time, and then type *d*, thus changing *as* to *ad*.

Space 1 time after a semicolon (but not before).

13 as←d; dadk←s; sas←d; laf←d; jal←k; sal←d; lasd←s;

Skillbuilding

I. WORD BUILDING

14 a ad ads; l la las lass; f fa fad; s sa sal sala;
15 d da dad; f fa fal fall; l la lad; j ja jas jass;

16 s sa sad; f fl fla flak; a as ask; s sa sas sass;
17 a ad add; a al alf alfa; j ja jak; a al ala alas;

J. 1-MINUTE TIMED WRITING

Take two 1-minute timed writings. Try to complete the passage each time. If you finish, press ENTER 2 times and start over again. The number scale below line 18 shows the number of words credited for typing a partial line. The software will automatically score your timed writings for speed and accuracy.

18 ask a sad lad; a fall fad; add a jak salad; a lad
      1 | 2 | 3 | 4 | 5 | 6 | 7 | 8 | 9 | 10

 **Goal:** At least 10wpm/1'/3e

 See "Introduction to the Student" at the front of your text for guidance on how speed and accuracy are measured.

Enrichment • Lesson 1

Type each line 2 times.

A. NEW-KEY REINFORCEMENT

1 a dads jass la daff ad add dak lad lads daks adds
2 ads fad lall lass fads alas alfa fala sad alfalfa

3 sal falda all fall sala as falls salad salsa flak
4 asks flask sass dad flasks skald dada jak ask lad

5 alas ask salads dads dak sala fad falda flask sal
6 alfalfa add fads all salad flak lass flask ads as

B. SHORT PHRASES

Type each phrase on a separate line; that is, press ENTER 1 time at the end of each line. Type each line 2 times; then press ENTER 2 times to insert a blank line between each line. Do not space after a semicolon if it is the last character on the line; instead, immediately after typing the semicolon, press ENTER.

7 a lad;
8 a lass;
9 a fall;

10 ask dad;
11 add all;
12 as a fad;

13 a fall ad;
14 dad falls;
15 jak salad;

16 add a lad;
17 ask a lass;
18 all flasks;

19 fall salads;
20 a lad asks dad;
21 a sad lass falls;

C. PARAGRAPH TYPING

First, type the following paragraph 1 time. Do not press ENTER at the end of each line; instead, let Word wrap end your lines for you. After you type the three lines 1 time, press ENTER 2 times and then type the three-line paragraph again.

22 fall salad; add a jak ad; alfalfa salad; ask a
23 sad lad; a lad asks dad; a lass asks dad; a sad
24 lad falls; a sad lad asks a dad; as a lass falls;

New Keys

Goals

- Touch-type the E, N, and T keys.
- Type at least 11wpm/1'/3e.

 Fingers are named for home-row keys. For example, the middle finger of the left hand is the D finger.

A. WARMUP

```
1  aa ss dd ff jj kk ll ;; fj dk sl a; asdf jkl; a;s
2  ask dad; a flask; a salsa salad; as sad as a lass
3  add salsa; fall fads; alas a sad lass; a dad; jak
```

 Tap the SPACE BAR with a downward and inward motion of your right thumb.

New Keys

B. NEW-KEY PROCEDURE

Follow this procedure when learning a new key:

1. Place your fingers on the home-row keys.
2. Look in the left margin of your lesson to see which finger controls the new key.
3. While looking at your keyboard and without actually typing, move the correct finger to the new key and back to home-row position. Do this several times—until you can make the reach without looking at your fingers.

4. Now, with your fingers still on the home-row keys, type the drill lines while keeping your eyes on the copy.
5. If you forget the location of a key, stop typing and repeat step 3.
6. You will make numerous errors while you are learning the keyboard; do not be overly concerned about them. Errors will decrease as you become more familiar with the keyboard.

C. THE E KEY

Keep the A finger at home as you reach for E.

Use the D finger.

```
 4   ddd ded ded ede ede eee alae dead eels fed jelled
 5   eke lead see fed fee safe eel ease seal deal dead
 6   deed feed jell keel lead seal elks fade leek seek
 7   a fake deal; feed a flea; lease a desk; sell ale;
```

D. THE N KEY

Keep the Sem finger at home as you reach for N.

Use the J finger.

```
 8   jjj jnj jnj njn njn nnn and sadness ends deafness
 9   knee kennel sneak an fan dens fen lens sedan lend
10   dean sane lane sank keen lens seen fend lank send
11   lend a needle; send jeans and sandals; needs land
```

E. THE T KEY

Keep the A finger at home as you reach for T.

Use the F finger.

```
12   fff ftf ftf tft tft ttt ate jet aft felt ant east
13   latte tat test at fat jest let ate late east daft
14   deft feet lent state taste tenet sets detest lets
15   a fast jet left at ten; staked a tent; tall tales
```

Skillbuilding

F. MINIMUM-CHANGE PRACTICE

Only one letter changes in each word.

```
16   lent sent send tend tent test nest lest fest jest
17   lake take tale tall tell fell felt feet feat seat
18   seed teed tend send sand land lend fend feed feel

19   lens tens fens fans tans tens dens dent lent sent
20   sank tank talk tale kale dale date late lane lank
21   jets lets less lass last fast fest feet feat seat
```

G. NEW-KEY REVIEW

E   22 easel deafen deed defeat defend delete dense ease
N   23 annals fanned kennel tenant tan and dean den fend
T   24 at attend attest detest estate fatten jest jetted

E   25 deaden dented detest eases eaten eel effete elate
N   26 keen land lend neat sent need net sedan seen send
T   27 tests kettle latent tent latest nettle tee settee

E   28 eke jested else ended estate fee lessee feed fete
N   29 tanned ant sense eaten knee sneak stand tend tent
T   30 settle state talent tan taste tenant tenet tsetse

H. CLAUSES

31 a tense staff deleted data; test a fast delta jet
32 a tenant dented a sedan; a sad tale ended at ten;
33 fasten a tan anklet; a lad ate a steak at a feast
34 a tall dean sat at a sedate settee; take an asset

I. 1-MINUTE TIMED WRITING

Take two 1-minute timed writings. Let word wrap end each line. Press ENTER only at the end of line 36.

 Goal: At least 11wpm/1'/3e

35 a tenant leased a fast jet and landed at a sedate   10
36 lake;   11

    1 | 2 | 3 | 4 | 5 | 6 | 7 | 8 | 9 | 10

Enrichment • Lesson 2

Type each line 2 times.

E
N
T

E
N
T

E
N
T

E N T
E N T
E N T

A. NEW-KEY REINFORCEMENT

1 fleet steel assets deafen lessee deed elate kneel
2 annals fanned nene anneal needle fennel leaden an
3 tats detest latest jet tsetse stats attest settle

4 detest lessen see leek skeet elands estate fallen
5 flan keen lean send knee sank land keen lane fend
6 aft let eta net alt fat sat ant ate set jet tanks

7 sleek leaden leaded needle easel knell sleets eke
8 and ant den end fan fen ken nee nets ten tan sane
9 settee state kettle tattle taste task kaftan test

10 nest detent tens sanest knelt neat teens dent net
11 tensed ante tanned talent sent nest latent fanjet
12 anklet tenant tend eaten attend assent ten fasten

Type each line 2 times.

⚠ Do not type the colored vertical lines that separate each phrase.

B. SHORT PHRASES

13 jet lease | sent fast | tan sedan | sent less | ten seats
14 dense lad | ten deeds | sent east | ten tasks | least tan
15 jet fleet | let feast | neat deal | neat feat | least sad

16 let stall | net leads | let stand | stale ale | let sneak
17 sent left | net deals | ten dates | sent data | ten lakes
18 ten desks | neat seat | ten deals | ate steak | let taste

Type each line 2 times.

C. CLAUSES

19 a teen ate at least ten dates and sat at a stand;
20 fasten a faded saddle and sandal at a sad estate;
21 a tall tan fanjet landed at a flat delta and sat;

22 all lasses tasted a lean steak and felt less sad;
23 a tenant sent kale salads and ate fat leeks fast;
24 a dad skated at a lake and leaned left at a tent;

25 take a seat at a settee and taste tea and salads;
26 a tall tenant leased a sedate teal sedan and sat;
27 at least a lad tasted steak and ale and ate fast;

New Keys

Goals

- Touch-type the O, R, and H keys.
- Type at least 12wpm/1′/3e.

A. WARMUP

learned keys   1   take a jet and taste a flat steak at a tall tent;

concentration   2   skedaddle attendant senseless flatlands steadfast

easy   3   an ant lent an elf a snake; an elk let an ant eat

New Keys

Keep the J finger at home as you reach for O.

Use the L finger.

B. THE O KEY

4   lll lol lol olo olo ooo do eons foe jot kook lots

5   no too so to not ton eon foe jot lot no dodo dojo

6   took soon solo onto oleo tool look foot fool soon

7   a felon loaded a lot of loose loot on an old lot;

Keep the A finger at home as you reach for R.

Use the F finger.

C. THE R KEY

8   fff frf frf rfr rfr rrr are drat erased fro okras

9   enroll ore errs tree rear ardor drear raked radar

10   erred rotor retro error rare rater rear errs dare

11   a red deer ran free for an area near a rear door;

Keep the Sem finger at home as you reach for H.

Use the J finger.

D. THE H KEY

12   jjj jhj jhj hjh hjh hhh ah adhere heh offhand shh

13   ankh oh rho she the ha he oh hah haha harsh heath

14   shah hallah the that she three here there her hot

15   she and he had heard that other short heron here;

Skillbuilding

Only one letter changes in each word.

E. MINIMUM-CHANGE PRACTICE

16 dash hash sash lash last lost host hoss loss less
17 hall tall tale kale hale hole role dole dolt jolt
18 hero here hare hard hark lark dark dank rank rant

19 jeer seer seek leek leak teak tear teal seal real
20 horn torn tort fort fore fare hare hard hart dart
21 heat seat feat fear hear sear dear dean lean leak

F. NEW-KEY REVIEW

O   22 food noon soon fool nook root solo tool donor oho
R   23 err rear ardor dares freer rarer roar order erred
H   24 hash hardhat harsher hath shah harsh heath hashed

O   25 foot odor toot oho drool oleo too hoof rook drool
R   26 radar raker rooter rare arrest reader rafter sort
H   27 heathen hashes health hearth hoorah heather trash

O   28 dodo lost toro doors onto flood hooks roof honors
R   29 errata orator darker render rather tartar terrors
H   30 rehash hothead sheath thrash thresh handheld hash

G. CLAUSES

31 she folded the sheets and he held her hands free;
32 he heard an oath and told her to note the reason;
33 the odd raft had floated onto the north seashore;
34 then she joked that he had stolen the old shades;
    1 | 2 | 3 | 4 | 5 | 6 | 7 | 8 | 9 | 10

H. 1-MINUTE TIMED WRITING

Take two 1-minute timed writings. Let word wrap end each line. Press ENTER only at the end of line 36.

35 the jaded steno learned a hard lesson on the trek   10
36 to a tree;   12
    1 | 2 | 3 | 4 | 5 | 6 | 7 | 8 | 9 | 10

 Goal: At least 12wpm/1'/3e

Enrichment • Lesson 3

Type each line 2 times.

A. NEW-KEY REINFORCEMENT

O

1 roost hotfoot solon forefoot loose offshoot odors
2 errs rater refer retro rotor harder roster resort
3 hardhats hasheesh hosanna hotshots rehashed flesh

4 nonfood shook forenoon stood torso onlooker hoots
5 darter terser horror roller eraser roarer errands
6 sheathed shoehorn aha thrasher handshake thrasher

7 shoot foothold forsooth noose stool rodeo tootles
8 narrator restorer tearjerker referral northerners
9 harshness horseshoe hotheaded shorthand threshold

10 rho ashore hoorah hero hereto shorts hoar hoarser
11 hoer holder hora horn honker forth horned shofars
12 frosh throes froth honor heron horror hoard honer

Column labels (left margin): O R H / O R H / H, and ORH ORH ORH for lines 10–12.

Type each line 2 times.

Do not type the colored vertical lines.

B. SHORT PHRASES

13 a loose shade|eats a short noodle|the rose thorns
14 a tattletale|she sat here|he often jostled a jerk
15 the rest of the lesson|thanks for the short looks

16 the oddest tattoos|those stolen forks|do not jerk
17 the shore floods|she flossed her teeth|jot a note
18 the earth shook hard|had a look|a tenth of a foot

Type each line 2 times.

C. CLAUSES

19 she shared her salad at the hotel near the shore;
20 three deer ran to the dark oak tree near the ark;
21 she had then also looked at the other ten horses;

22 she set all of the stolen art on that tall shelf;
23 take a seat near the dark settee and talk to her;
24 the teal sandals on her feet had soon fallen off;

25 the loose earth on the north and east had fallen;
26 ask her not to take the nonfat food to the stall;
27 the senator held a safe seat and soon left there;

New Keys

4

Goals

- Touch-type the I, Left Shift, and Period keys.
- Type at least 13wpm/1′/3e.

A. WARMUP

learned keys	1	the soda jerks fell onto a stall and told a joke;
concentration	2	horseshoe northeast shorthand therefore threshold
easy	3	half of an oak had torn and also half of a shelf;

New Keys

Keep the J finger at home as you reach for I.

Use the K finger.

B. THE I KEY

```
4  kkk kik kik iki iki iii aid die lei fit hit radii
5  jilt kid lit nit oil rid sits tie id if in is ilk
6  aid sin did fie kid jail kid lid nil tie oils ail
7  nine irises in a lei did die in a sink in a deli;
```

Use the A finger.

C. THE LEFT SHIFT KEY

To capitalize letters on the right half of the keyboard:

1. With the F finger at home, press and hold down the Left Shift key with the A finger.

2. Press the letter key to be capitalized.

3. Immediately release the Left Shift key and return fingers to the home-row position.

```
 8  aaa Jaa Jaa Kaa Kaa Laa Laa Naa Iaa Oaa Jane Hank
 9  Hans Hale Jade Jake Ian Kate Nan Oak Ian Hal Lara
10  Nan Halle Ian Karl Lara Lena Oates Jan Katie Lars
11  Neither Jake Hanks nor Nathan Karl is in Oakland;
```

Keep the J finger at home as you reach for the period.

Use the L finger.

D. THE ⬛ KEY

Follow these rules for spacing with periods:

- Do not space before a period.
- Space 1 time after a period following an abbreviation.
- Do not space after a period within an abbreviation.
- Space 1 time after each initial in a person's name.

- Space 1 time after a period ending a sentence in the middle of a paragraph. Do *not* space after a period at the end of a paragraph.

```
12  lll l.l l.l .l. .l. ... i.e. addl. intl. n.d. Jr.
13  Jan. Ill. a.k.a. N.J. Ind. anon. asst. N.H. Okla.
14  No. et al. i.e. I did. He is not. Ian ate. I sat.
15  J. L. Harris is in Okla. or Ill. for addl. tasks.
```

Skillbuilding

E. MINIMUM-CHANGE PRACTICE

```
16  sink link fink find kind kink link rink rind kind
17  file tile till kill sill silk silt lilt tilt tint
18  fail tail sail said laid lair hair hail nail rail

19  sill kill fill fall Falk talk tall Hall Hill Jill
20  list fist fish dish dash Nash Nast fast last Lash
21  Jane Lane Kane Kant rant rent Lent lint tint hint
```

F. NEW-KEY REVIEW

I

LEFT SHIFT

.

I LEFT SHIFT .

```
22  idiot initial kiddie raisin finish initiate if in
23  John Hall Lisa Jane Olaf Jill Joan Lois Joel Koto
24  H. I. J. K. L. N. O. n.d. Jr. i.e. No. Jan. asst.
25  Ida J. Harris; Indira K. Little; Lillian N. Iris;
```

G. SENTENCES

26 Neither Iris L. Harris nor Ida N. Jones is there.
27 In Orlando he had the aid of Nikita to finish it.
28 Lillian H. Little did not hide it inside the tin.
29 Inlaid tiles are on Oak Lane for Kristina to see.
       1 | 2 | 3 | 4 | 5 | 6 | 7 | 8 | 9 | 10

H. 1-MINUTE TIMED WRITING

30 Lisa N. Jenkins had dined in Oakland. Lois had   10
31 to find her there.   13
       1 | 2 | 3 | 4 | 5 | 6 | 7 | 8 | 9 | 10

Take two 1-minute timed writings.

Goal: At least 13wpm/1'/3e

Enrichment • Lesson 4

Type each line 2 times.

I

LEFT SHIFT

.

I

LEFT SHIFT

.

I

LEFT SHIFT

.

I LEFT SHIFT .
I LEFT SHIFT .
I LEFT SHIFT .

Type each line 2 times.

Type each line 2 times.

A. NEW-KEY REINFORCEMENT

1 aid air din fir fit hit ilk ink inn ire iris this
2 Joe Kid Les Ian Ned Ida Noe Lil Jon Ira Kent John
3 a.k.a. addl. Okla. N.J. N.H. n.d. intl. asst. Jr.

4 lid ail did fit tin tie sin oil irk if it is in I
5 Lee Joe Ida Ina Joel Leo John Koto Olaf I. N. Jai
6 anon. et al. i.e. Ill. Ind. Jan. n.d. No. Ltd. H.

7 idea iris nail dial edit into file sink soil hint
8 Jill Lisa Nina Lois Hall Jane Joel Hart Olaf Joan
9 I. J. K. L. N. O. Joe. H. Nie; Leo K. Kale; L. J.

10 Keith N. Harris; Irene I. Olson; Katie O. Hinder;
11 Hilario I. Oleans; Kristen N. Jai; Leila N. Jain;
12 Keiko O. Ikeda; Ida H. Jenkins; Lillie N. Little;

B. SHORT PHRASES

13 that diet soda; an inlaid tile; finish the tasks;
14 tried to aid her; a dirt floor; I. I. Johnson Jr.
15 initial on the fifth line; it is OK; hire Ida Li;

16 a fair deal; a kosher deli; kiss the thin kiddie;
17 other ideas; tidied the dens; inside this raisin;
18 H. and I. and J. and K. and L. and N. and O.; OK;

C. SENTENCES

19 Olla needs to freshen the tired look of the nook.
20 Keith did not find the softened toast in the tin.
21 I think either N.H. or N.J. is OK for the hotels.

22 Leo Jones insisted on the three lessons in there.
23 Iris Joel had fished here and had liked it a lot.
24 Leila sifted and stirred the soil that needed it.

25 Lois N. Henderson is a dentist there in Lakeland.
26 Ina has to attend the initial session in Oakland.
27 Jill had not finished the task so I assisted her.

New Keys

Goals

- Touch-type the B, U, and C keys.
- Type at least 14wpm/1′/3e.

A. WARMUP

learned keys	1	Jake Nort had not led a fast life; he had rested.
concentration	2	Hadassah Henderson Jonathan Jeanette Leonardo Lee
easy	3	Keith Idle and Henri did tie a fish to the dials.

New Keys

B. THE B KEY

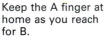

Keep the A finger at home as you reach for B.

Use the F finger.

4   fff fbf fbf bfb bfb bbb label ebbs tidbits rebels
5   offbeat bib inkblot alb inbred job orb hotbed lab
6   babes barbs bobbin blab babble blob bobbed bobble
7   His best baseball and bat are near a blond table.

C. THE U KEY

Keep the Sem finger at home as you reach for U.

Use the J finger.

8   jjj juj juj uju uju uuu tau but dun euro fun huts
9   radius jut kudos flu nut out run sub tub flu aunt
10   luaus lulu tutus dufus undue usual bureau unusual
11   Kudos to Luke for the debut of his book on burns.

D. THE C KEY

Keep the A finger at home as you reach for C.

Use the D finger.

12   ddd dcd dcd cdc cdc ccc aces bobcat occur redcoat
13   deck ashcan ice bookcase talc inch dock arc discs
14   etch duck etch buck doc arc chic cacti cubic cock
15   Our church choirs can cancel our recitals on cue.

Skillbuilding

E. MINIMUM-CHANGE PRACTICE

16 buck luck lock rock rack race lace late Kate Kane
17 cube tube tune tone tine tint hint hind hand hard
18 curb carb cart dart dark lark Lars bars cars care

19 bout boat coat coal foal foul four tour hour sour
20 cure cute lute lube tube tune tone hone hose nose
21 bare barn bard lard lord cord curd card hard hark

F. NEW-KEY REVIEW

B
U
C
B U C

22 baker banjo bark basin bribe brake bond boast bit
23 unit uke urn use fuel hulk sun tusk house duo sub
24 cab chat carol chili check church condo cell aces
25 cub buck curb scuba scrub biscuit cubicle cutback

G. SENTENCES

26 Joe and Lee think the surf and turf is delicious.
27 Kent said a bunch of bandits robbed a local bank.
28 Unit costs of the industrial knob are reasonable.
29 Nine of the jurors can render the decisions soon.

H. 1-MINUTE TIMED WRITING

Take two 1-minute timed writings.

Goal: At least 14wpm/1'/3e

30 Her old brick condo near Lake Huron has just the   10
31 features Luis needed.   14
   1 | 2 | 3 | 4 | 5 | 6 | 7 | 8 | 9 | 10

Enrichment • Lesson 5

A. NEW-KEY REINFORCEMENT

Type each line 2 times.

B
U
C

1 bans bar bud rib fib bad bin bat bee job ebb labs
2 dub jut run rubs sue but bud ours dud bun fur due
3 act can aces cab cat cod cot cad ice con cuts cue

B
U
C

4 babe debt bank able book snub blob boat both stab
5 euro haul Luke hush loud feud cure sour foul husk
6 ache duck cent each Nick cake inch fact lack care

B
U
C

7 abode board tribe boast beret burros brake rabbis
8 fruits audit crush abuse routes found ruler adult
9 catch crude acute clicks cross check chosen black

B U C
B U C
B U C

10 because buck butcher cube curb scuba subject club
11 cutback cubic cherub bucket biscuit bounce buckle
12 cubicle obscure brunch cubs curable scrub bunches

B. SHORT PHRASES

Type each line 2 times.

13 a brisk canter; because of us; a bunch of bananas
14 a rude subject; a tribe of Indians; choke a horse
15 the color of chalk; adults and children; a cherub

16 the noble cause; cost a fortune; a crust of bread
17 a unit of blood, a bleak outlook; hurt just a bit
18 black belt in karate; blue suede shoes; fur coats

C. SENTENCES

Type each line 2 times.

19 Little obscure cutbacks did not affect their job.
20 Her old cubicle is near the corner of the office.
21 Jack had a bacon biscuit and cola for his brunch.

22 Jed beat the odds because the disease is curable.
23 Haul the bucket of nuts and bolts to the shelter.
24 Look for the subject of the broken link to arise.

25 Just fill in the blank line and send it all back.
26 His adobe house near our house has not been sold.
27 One black briefcase is on the bureau in the hall.

Keyboarding: The Alphabet

LESSON 6
New Keys: RIGHT SHIFT W M

LESSON 7
New Keys: X P TAB

LESSON 8
New Keys: Q , G

LESSON 9
New Keys: V Y Z

LESSON 10
Review

New Keys

Goals

- Touch-type the RIGHT SHIFT, W, and M keys.
- Type at least 15wpm/1′/3e.

A. WARMUP

learned keys
concentration
speed

1 Her brief research could land Kate her first job.
2 abundance incurable obstructs bucketful clubhouse
3 Keith has both an auto and a bus but is not rich.

New Keys

Use the Sem finger.

B. THE RIGHT [SHIFT] KEY

To capitalize letters on the left half of the keyboard:

1. With the J finger at home, press and hold down the RIGHT SHIFT key with the Sem finger.
2. Press the letter key to be capitalized.
3. Immediately release the RIGHT SHIFT key and return fingers to the home-row position.

4 ;;; A;; S;; D;; F;; Ali Sol Don Fido Eli Todd Ron
5 Burr Cora Bo Che Alan Dick Sue Dot Chris Rob Ruth
6 Bob Ana Don Blake Diane Bud Ann Rufus Rod Al Elon
7 Diane S. Dickens likes the East Coast of Florida.

Use the S finger.

C. THE [W] KEY

8 sss sws sws wsw wsw www bawls cobwebs dwarf fewer
9 thwart kiwi awkward bulwark unwed owe Darwin swab
10 two Kuwait bowwow owls news laws ewe haw how owns
11 Wanda went to the World Wide Web for the lowdown.

Use the J finger.

D. THE [M] KEY

12 jjj jmj jmj mjm mjm mmm am submit acme admit hems
13 Hoffman ohm him Hackman calm ammo unmet moms arms
14 ism Batman hums Newman Emma maim memos mime madam
15 Mamie can make a commitment to the mammal museum.

Skillbuilding

E. WORD BUILDING

16 A Al Ala Alan; D Do Don; R Ru Rut Ruth; m mu mum;
17 m mo mow; w wa war warm; M Ma Mac; w wh who whom;
18 m ma mai maim; e el elm; a ar arm; M Ma Mam Mama;

19 a ai aim; o oh ohm; s sw swa swam; T To Tod Todd;
20 M Mo Mom; w wh who whom; w wo wor worm; w wa war;
21 E Em Emm Emma; m ma mar; w wa war warm; M Mi Mia;

F. NEW-KEY REVIEW

RIGHT SHIFT   22 Adam Walt Carl Emma Rick Taft Ward Tate Rita Eric
W   23 news wire dawn owls wish awes dews town wake wolf
M   24 mill name demo home mast mind dime mini omen dome

RIGHT SHIFT   25 Will Aida Chad Erie Rome Tara Tess Ross Ewan Weir
W   26 wood twin bows bowl slaw know webs wool flaw claw
M   27 item mate mint room stem miss jamb dorm ammo lamb

RIGHT SHIFT   28 Alan Alma Webb Fern Ruhr Thad West Theo Fiji Cuba
W   29 fowl stew work stow whom crew wife crow wall wind
M   30 math mist team lima drum arms limo mean term monk

G. 1-MINUTE TIMED WRITING

Take two 1-minute timed writings. Press ENTER only at the end of line 32.

Goal: At least 15wpm/1'/3e

31 Then Barbra just left them at the house since the   10
32 men and women were awake.   15
      1 | 2 | 3 | 4 | 5 | 6 | 7 | 8 | 9 | 10

Enrichment • Lesson 6

Type each line 2 times.

RIGHT SHIFT
W
M

RIGHT SHIFT
W
M

RIGHT SHIFT
W
M

RIGHT SHIFT W M
RIGHT SHIFT W M
RIGHT SHIFT W M

A. NEW-KEY REINFORCEMENT

1 Anne Arab Dade Finn Sara Thor Tito Saul Fisk Dale
2 arrow crown dews word watch awe water towel award
3 aim number him album human dam alumni amend dream

4 Asia Wolf Baja Dana Ford Scot Toto Will Seth Demi
5 owner we row drawl bow elbow brawl towel who when
6 sum mob me arm elm macro aroma female month woman

7 Barb Bess Dodd Adam Shaw Finn Dean Shea Webb Earl
8 jewel waist straw law swine crowd war allow drown
9 man method Ms. mud crime hum admit am amuse armed

10 Awesome Somehow Swims Warmer Winsome Wisdom Warms
11 Twosome Swami Warmed Cutworm Dimwit Swarm Walkman
12 Wartime Snowman Woman Welcomes Swimmer Whom Women

Type each line 2 times.

B. SHIFT KEY PRACTICE

13 Jack Neal Shea Nell Jane Alan Dodd Jean Nero Jeff
14 Earl Alma Anne Ella Emil Thad Theo Emma Oahu Thor
15 Tito Kane Kate Kent Fiji Bill Finn Ural Bonn Fisk

16 Otto Urdu Ford Owen Uris Utah Fuji Laos Utes Rice
17 Hank Hans Rick Rita Hera Herb Mack Mali Chad Chen
18 Marc Wild Will Mari Cook Cuba Matt Wolf Wood Mead

C. SENTENCES

19 Mr. Taft admitted that his claim was turned down.
20 Ms. Wu used her Web cam and also browsed the Web.
21 Blossoms bloom when it rains twice in four weeks.
22 I wasted much time when I was in town last month.

Type each paragraph 2 times, letting word wrap end each line for you.

D. PARAGRAPH TYPING

23 Ms. Cara Fields listed Milwaukee Tech as her alma   10
24 mater on her resume. I think that she majored in   20
25 business administration and minored in science.   29

26 We rode in a sleek limousine from the hotel to   9
27 Jackson Hole and ate dinner at the Camelback   19
28 Restaurant. We both ordered seafood and wine.   28

29 The newest member of our firm is Ms. Caroline K.   10
30 Smith; she will start work tomorrow as our labor   20
31 relations assistant and will work in New Hall.   29

        1 | 2 | 3 | 4 | 5 | 6 | 7 | 8 | 9 | 10

New Keys

Goals

- Touch-type the X, P, and TAB keys.
- Type at least 16wpm/1'/3e.

A. WARMUP

learned keys   1 Ask Al and Jan to be in the room with Ms. Fuchs.
alternate hand   2 rituals socials downtown anthems dorms authentic
speed   3 Chris has to make an enamel dish for the mantel.

New Keys

Use the S finger.

B. THE X KEY

4 sss sxs sxs xsx xsx xxx ax ox fox box tax fix mix
5 axis jinx crux exam taxi exit hoax text coax flex
6 next lax inbox index sexism exhaust exists deluxe
7 The next wax exhibit will excite the anxious fox.

Use the Sem finger.

C. THE P KEY

8 ;;; ;p; ;p; p;p p;p ppp pi ape subplot mudpie pep
9 ashpit pips inkpad helps imps input opt apps warp
10 spa output up cowpea pa Alp top apes cap map cops
11 Pat put up a pinup that he ripped from the paper.

Use the A finger.

D. THE TAB KEY

The TAB key is used to indent paragraphs 0.5 inch. As shown on the next page, you can also align words in columns by pressing the TAB key.

Keep your F finger in home-row position as you quickly press the TAB key, and return your A finger to home-row position immediately after you press the TAB key.

Press TAB when you see the → symbol.

```
12  aah→  abs→  ace→  act→  add→  ado→  ads→  aft→  aha
13  aid→  ail→  aim→  air→  ale→  all→  alt→  amp→  and
14  ant→  ape→  app→  apt→  arc→  are→  ark→  arm→  art
15  ash→  ask→  asp→  ate→  auk→  awe→  awl→  awn→  axe
```

Skillbuilding

E. WORD BUILDING

```
16  p pr pro prop; b bo box; p pa pac pack; s se sex;
17  p pa pad; e ex exa exam; p pe pep; e ex exi exit;
18  f fo fox; p pi pin pint; p pa par part; w wa wax;

19  j ji jin jinx; r ra rap; p pi pin; t te tex text;
20  p po por port; f fi fix; p pl pla plan; m mi mix;
21  o op opt; f fl fle flex; p pu put; c co coa coax;
```

F. NEW-KEY REVIEW

X   22 box exile apex exec minx fox boxers ox inbox flux
P   23 pack dope pair ripe pest wipe plan sped jeep shop
TAB   24 is→ no→ on→ to→ we→ in→ he→ be→ at

X   25 expo wax next sax axed excess oxen maxi axle taxi
P   26 pain spam park upon pile bump plot apex camp whip
TAB   27 ad→ as→ do→ hi→ if→ it→ of→ or→ up

X   28 excuse tax expense reflex textbook except mailbox
P   29 palm hope part stop pine cope poem kept wrap deep
TAB   30 us→ so→ oh→ me→ id→ ho→ ha→ an→ am

G. 1-MINUTE TIMED WRITING

Take two 1-minute timed writings. Press ENTER only at the end of line 32.

 **Goal:** At least 16wpm/1'/3e

Note: The word counts in this book credit you with 1 stroke for each paragraph indention in a timed writing. The timed writing starts when you press the TAB key.

```
31       Just ask the six of them to wait in place        9
32  for Brenda to complete that last job.                16
     1  |  2  |  3  |  4  |  5  |  6  |  7  |  8  |  9  | 10
```

Enrichment • Lesson 7

A. NEW-KEY REINFORCEMENT

Type each line 2 times.

X
1 execute fixture exercise excuse mailbox exert tax
P
2 paper piper pauper prop pompom peep pope pulp pop
TAB
3 at→ is→ ho→ on→ to→ up→ in→ he→ be

X
4 lax maximum annex exception inexact examine extra
P
5 people pulpit pupil puppies pepper pump pinup opt
TAB
6 an→ as→ do→ hi→ if→ it→ of→ or→ we

X
7 example exclude experience except experts excuses
P
8 puppet pipe poplar up slipup rapper supper tiptop
TAB
9 us→ no→ so→ oh→ me→ id→ ha→ ad→ am

X, P, TAB
10 max→ mix→ cop→ tax→ pit→ pro→ pox→ hip→ lap
X, P, TAB
11 ape→ pad→ box→ cap→ fix→ pod→ cup→ tip→ rap
X, P, TAB
12 pep→ lax→ pet→ sip→ fox→ pun→ sax→ map→ wax

B. CORRESPONDING-FINGER PRACTICE

Type each line 2 times.

A and Sem
13 abase; fatal; axial; afar; area; ahead; ajar; Al;
S and L
14 else slap lets self list oils also lose last slam
W and O
15 word blow down owes flow show know whom crow work

D and K
16 dark dike eked kind deck kids disk skid desk duck
E and I
17 edit line bite nice bike side ripe cite tire deli
R and U
18 rule true burn sour four rule ours curb sure hour

C. SENTENCES

19 Paul was anxious to drop off the box of old maps.
20 The extra income Pam earned is exempt from taxes.
21 People expect excellent results on their laptops.
22 Please exit the plane and step on the purple box.

D. PARAGRAPH TYPING

Type each paragraph 2 times.

23   Just a few taxis were on the roads on that   9
24 black and cold late afternoon. I needed a map to   19
25 find the street to the second job consultation.   28

26   Blake used his own expertise to prepare the   9
27 report on the success of the annual fall flower   19
28 show. He reported that the show was a major hit.   28

29   We mixed up the names in random order so   8
30 that no one could know when he or she would be   18
31 called on to strum the banjo for the audience.   27

   1 | 2 | 3 | 4 | 5 | 6 | 7 | 8 | 9 | 10

New Keys

Goals

- Touch-type the Q, Comma, and G keys.
- Type at least 17wpm/1'/3e.

A. WARMUP

learned keys 1 Ned Black spotted the four women at that jukebox.
one hand   2 best jump card noun debt mink base pump read upon
speed   3 Six of their chaps spent their profit in Orlando.

New Keys

Use the A finger.

B. THE Q KEY

4 aaa aqa aqa qaq qaq qqq aquas acquit equals pique
5 kumquat banquet croquet torque squad bouquet quip
6 quad quid pique quaff equip quiet quit quack quod
7 Quin quoted from his unique request for a quorum.

Use the K finger.

C. THE , KEY

Space 1 time after a comma (but not before). However, do not space after a punctuation mark or word that ends a line; instead, immediately press ENTER.

8 kkk k,k k,k ,k, ,k, ,,, ma, cab, arc, ad, be, of,
9 oh, ask, Al, am, pin, too, up, ore, is, eat, emu,
10 ho, box; Al, Bo, Ed, Jo, Di, or I; a, b, c, or d;
11 Li, Ed, and I wrote, proofread, and formatted it.

Use the F finger.

D. THE G KEY

12 fff fgf fgf gfg gfg ggg ages edge begs afghan egg
13 dig ginkgo alga Eng cog popgun urge disgust outgo
14 bug gag gang gouge aging gongs gauge gorged going
15 Greg Rigg is going to see ping pong in Hong Kong.

Skillbuilding

E. BACKSPACE-KEY PRACTICE

Type each word as shown until you reach the backspace sign (←). Then backspace 1 time and replace the previously typed character with the one shown; for example, in line 16, *gale* becomes *gall*.

```
16  gale←l at←n gag←p had←m he←i bad←n if←n ad←h or←n
17  gut←n mask←h big←n me←u her←m dire←k slaw←p age←o
18  us←p die←m as←n box←o of←h kit←n hut←m mad←n it←n
```

F. NEW-KEY REVIEW

Q
,
G

Q
,
G

Q
,
G

```
19  banquet quotas squalor square quote quail bouquet
20  ago, rub, can, pop, jag, lax, men, owe, air, fun,
21  blog sign gold sing drag edge good wing gain high

22  liquid quid request squid quark queen clique quit
23  one, lag, ton, aid, sex, two, ear, jar, use, new,
24  logo rage cage glad ring huge guru long urge gate

25  croquet quarrel sequel quilt quarter equator quip
26  own, aim, ten, let, cap, its, our, ask, kin, bad,
27  goal king glow golf wage drug grow page grew gift
```

G. SENTENCES

```
28  Gus was quick to go to Quebec, Canada, in August.
29  He began to quarrel, argue, and quibble about it.
30  Gosh, Peg sighed at the quietness at the equator.

31  Bring the unique graph, ledger, and plaques here.
32  Grace brought a gold liqueur to the golf banquet.
33  Megan quit using that croquet equipment long ago.
```

H. 1-MINUTE TIMED WRITING

Take two 1-minute timed writings.

Goal: At least 17wpm/1'/3e

```
34       Just ask Phil to quit making that big racket      9
35  and, in addition, to fix the wood pipe.               17
      1 | 2 | 3 | 4 | 5 | 6 | 7 | 8 | 9 | 10
```

Enrichment • Lesson 8

A. NEW-KEY REINFORCEMENT

Type each line 2 times.

Q
,
G

1 equals quirk squid quote quest squat unique quick
2 ajar, jeeps, jump, joke, joins, jerk, junk, just,
3 agents range align cargo right guides judge globe

Q
,
G

4 squad quits equip quads liquid quiet square quota
5 book, kick, kind, like, risks, pack, neck, keeps,
6 grants light fight angles grasp great dough agree

Q
,
G

7 quarts quilt squab queen quips squeal quail quite
8 apex, oxen, taxi, coax, jinx, axles, text, exams,
9 gains begins images grade might doing being greed

B. VERTICAL REACHES

Type each line 2 times.

Up Reaches

10 at atlas match later plate water batch fatal late
11 dr drums draft drift drawn drain drama dress drab
12 ju jumps juror junks jumbo julep judge juice just

Down Reaches

13 ca cadet cable cabin camel cameo cards carts cash
14 nk trunk drink prank rinks brink drank crank sink
15 ba baked batch badge bagel banjo barge basis bank

C. ROW PRACTICE

Type each line 2 times.

Top Row

16 We were to take our trucks to Pete at the window.
17 There were two tired people at the hut in Warsaw.
18 Please write to their home to tell Tom in a week.

Home Row

19 Jake asked his dad for small red flags in Dallas.
20 She is glad he added a dash of salt to the salad.
21 Dale said she sold her glasses at that fall sale.

Bottom Row

22 He can come to the annex in Macon to meet Maxine.
23 Their maximum number from Mexico can come to box.
24 Mabel Baxter connected with the Nixons in Benson.

New Keys

Goals

- Touch-type the V, Y, and Z keys.
- Type at least 18wpm/1'/3e.

A. WARMUP

learned keys   1   The quick boxing warden jumped and flipped sides.

one hand   2   were lion card hump base join feat hook axes hulk

speed   3   A half bushel of corn was thrown to the big duck.

New Keys

Use the F finger.

B. THE V KEY

4   fff fvf fvf vfv vfv vvv avows obvious advice even

5   five salve Humvee anvil doves curved outvoted luv

6   vie event Van vat vie vexes vim vet vow via vivid

7   Eva and Vi visited the vast civic event in Provo.

Use the J finger.

C. THE Y KEY

8   jjj jyj jyj yjy yjy yyy aye by icy dyes eyes defy

9   gym shy sky fly my any boys spy cry busy sty guys

10   ivy dewy sexy buy guy joy pay way yes yew you yet

11   Kelly may buy the forty gray kayaks for the navy.

Use the A finger.

D. THE Z KEY

12   aaa aza aza zaz zaz zzz daze subzero czar adz fez

13   zigzagged biz unzip cozy ditz ouzo frowzy analyze

14   buzz pizzazz fuzzy jazz abuzz zit gaze razzmatazz

15   Zeke rented a cozy Mazda from Hertz in the plaza.

Skillbuilding

E. SPACE BAR PRACTICE

Space without pausing.

16 a b c d e f g h i j k l m n o p q r s t u v w xyz
17 an as be by go in is it me no of or to we ad Al I
18 ah am at do he hi but id if ma my on so up us for

19 Do not go to Ada or Ida for work every day or so.
20 I am sure he can go with you if he has some time.
21 He is to be at the car by the time you get there.

F. NEW-KEY REVIEW

V	22	cove gave vane love vein ever verb vast avow oven
Y	23	army ally city many copy navy gray away yell only
Z	24	buzz whiz gaze quiz zinc fez zeal fizzy zany daze

V	25	dove five vain diva over vest have vote vent move
Y	26	clay envy baby type Tony hype pays myth pony easy
Z	27	lazy ooze zips zero size daze Hazel zoo zoom jazz

V	28	five save even view dive veto void live vine avid
Y	29	busy lady play typo body holy defy nosy vary boxy
Z	30	gaze zest hazy cozy zone zaps ziti haze wiz dozen

G. SENTENCES

31 Hazel gave Zeke some advice on verbs and adverbs.
32 You really need to try out your new frozen pizza.
33 Forty or fifty of you have yet to give any money.

34 I eyed the dazzling piece made of topaz and onyx.
35 You have to visit my newest exhibit in Las Vegas.
36 Zelda vividly gazed at the ritzy piazza in Provo.

H. 1-MINUTE TIMED WRITING

Take two 1-minute timed writings.

Goal: At least 18wpm/1'/3e

37	David quickly spotted those four old women	9
38	who were just dozing over in the new jury box.	18

1 | 2 | 3 | 4 | 5 | 6 | 7 | 8 | 9 | 10

Enrichment • Lesson 9

A. NEW-KEY REINFORCEMENT

Type each line 2 times.

V 1 cover value level movie never drive advice clever
Y 2 bylaw entry money every angry needy anyway typify
Z 3 craze seize klutz unzip dizzy zesty zealot wizard

V 4 grave valid avoid solve rival voice device avenue
Y 5 lucky annoy maybe decay imply dirty heyday yearly
Z 6 pizza dozen razor blaze ritzy hazel guzzle sizzle

V 7 cover prove never event leave civic behave divide
Y 8 decoy hurry carry glory diary empty byways mayday
Z 9 ozone prize amaze zebra gauze froze puzzle nozzle

B. COMMON LETTER COMBINATIONS

Type each line 2 times.

Word Beginnings

10 comply comedy combat coming common commit compels
11 forget forbid forced forest formal former formats
12 permit perils peruse perish period person peruses
13 subtle submit subdue subtly suburb sublet subways

Word Endings

14 enable liable nimble edible doable usable jumbles
15 joyful fitful useful armful sinful lawful boxfuls
16 caring typing losing hiring seeing having rulings
17 action option notion vision region nation motions

C. PARAGRAPH TYPING

Type each paragraph 2 times.

18   Back in July, we were authorized to acquire   9
19 five boxes of green letterhead stationery. That   19
20 amount should be ample for the entire year.   27

21   Kate took a quick jet to Phoenix, Arizona,   9
22 to enjoy the weather and to have time to begin   19
23 fall duties with the Girl Scouts of America.   27

24   Please just fix the copier quickly so that   9
25 we can minimize our downtime and get productivity   19
26 back in shape. We have to meet our monthly quota.   29

     1 | 2 | 3 | 4 | 5 | 6 | 7 | 8 | 9 | 10

Review

10

Goals

- Reinforce key reaches.
- Type at least 19wpm/1'/3e.

A. WARMUP

alphabet	1	Five boxing wizards jumped quickly into the ring.
shift keys	2	Mr. Ho and Ms. Yu let Al, Bo, Ed, Jo, and Ty eat.
speed	3	Dick may air the new anthem on the eighth of May.

Skillbuilding

B. REVIEW: A–D

4 alpaca acacia banana cabana armada azalea pajamas
5 Bob bobbin babble bubble blubber bumblebee bobble
6 Cy cyclic concentric eclectic climactic eccentric
7 do added daddy addled nodded doodad dodged kidded

C. REVIEW: E–H

8 epees eerie emcees geese levee peeve tepee beeper
9 fisticuffs fluffy foodstuff liftoff falloff fluff
10 groggy eggnog giggle baggage gauging digging gigs
11 hitchhike high hashish hashes highlight Chihuahua

D. REVIEW: I–L

12 idiotic bikini if illicit inhibit initial militia
13 jobs jog jam jar jaws jay jet jig jut jog jot joy
14 kick kinky kook knock key kayak khaki kiosk knack
15 lull locally fulfill loyally lullaby ill billfold

E. REVIEW: M–P

16 mommy mammal mummy mammoth medium maximum minimum
17 nanny cannon inning antenna canning pennant ninny
18 outdoor outlook offshoot option onlooker orthodox
19 peppy poppy puppies pepper popped puppets propped

F. REVIEW: Q–T

20 quip aqua equal quay quid equip quip quit Quakers
21 rarer errors horror mirror terror arrears barrier
22 sass sissy Swiss assess says assets assist senses
23 tattoo attest tattle attempt tilt attract statute

G. REVIEW: U–X

24 unusual gurus usurious luau luxurious sunup undue
25 valve viva savvy verve vivid evolve revive velvet
26 widows willow window awkward swallow wows walkway
27 ax ox box fix fox hex lax mix nix sax sex tax tux

H. REVIEW: Y–Z, COMMA, PERIOD

28 yearly byway gypsy pygmy shyly anyway payday your
29 zigzag buzz pizzazz jazz fuzzy pizza buzzer zesty
30 am, we, in, is up, an, to, be, no, do, my, go, it
31 Mr. Ms. Dr. Mrs. Esq. Inc. pp. Nos. Wed. Oct. Pa.

I. 1-MINUTE TIMED WRITING

Take two 1-minute timed writings.

 Goal: At least 19wpm/1´/3e

32   Back in June, we delivered oxygen equipment   9
33 of odd sizes to the new hospital near Ogden,   18
34 Utah.   19

   1 | 2 | 3 | 4 | 5 | 6 | 7 | 8 | 9 | 10

Enrichment • Lesson 10

Type each line 2 times.

A. REVIEW: A–E

1 Allan asked Alma Adams to fly to Alaska and Asia.
2 Both Barbara and Robb bought a rubber basketball.
3 Carly can accept a classic car at a Cairo clinic.
4 Dade suddenly dined in the dark diner in Detroit.
5 Reeves said Eddie edited the entire eleven texts.

Type each line 2 times.

B. REVIEW: F–J

6 Five friars focused on the four offensive fables.
7 George gave the bag of green grapes to Gina Gaye.
8 Haughty Hugh hoped Hal had helped Seth with this.
9 Iris liked to pickle pickles in the acidic brine.
10 Jo Jones joined a junior jogging team in pajamas.

Type each line 2 times.

C. REVIEW: K–O

11 Ken kept a sleek kayak for the ski trek to Akron.
12 Luella played a well-planned ball game in Lowell.
13 I made more money on many markups of the pompoms.
14 Ned and Ginny knew ten men in a main dining room.
15 Opal Orr opened four boxes of oranges at the zoo.

Type each line 2 times.

D. REVIEW: P–T

16 Pat paid to park the plane at the pump in Pompey.
17 Quincy quickly quit his quarterly quiz in Quebec.
18 Robin carried four rare rulers into that library.
19 Sam signed, sealed, and sent six leases to Jesse.
20 Matt caught the little trout near Twelfth Street.

Type each line 2 times.

E. REVIEW: U–Z

21 Uncle Rubin urged Judy to go see a guru in Utica.
22 Vivian moved to veto five voice votes in Ventura.
23 Walt waited while Wilma went to Watts for a week.
24 Alexi mixed sixty extra extracts exactly as told.
25 Yes, your young son plays cymbals anyway at Yale.
26 Liza saw the zany zebras zigzag in the Ozark zoo.

        1 | 2 | 3 | 4 | 5 | 6 | 7 | 8 | 9 | 10

Keyboarding: Numbers and Symbols

New Keys

Goals

- Touch-type the -, 2, and 9 keys.
- Type at least 19wpm/2′/5e.

A. WARMUP

alphabet	1	Big July earthquakes confounded the zany experimental vows.
concentration	2	uncommunicativeness departmentalization electrocardiography
easy	3	It is the duty of the busy ensigns to dismantle the panels.

New Keys

Keep the J finger in home-row position.

Use the Sem finger.

B. THE - KEY

Do not space before or after a hyphen.

```
 4   ;;; ;p; ;-; ;-; -;- -;- --- no-no to-do mix-up run-in X-ray
 5   pop-up sit-in add-on get-go set-to can-do U-turn up-to-date
 6   Jo Dye-Lee, a well-to-do jack-of-all-trades, had a boo-boo.
 7   Le-Sam is a shut-in who drank a pick-me-up from the get-go.
```

Keep either the A or F finger in home-row position.

Use the S finger.

C. THE 2 KEY

```
 8   sss sws s2s s2s 2s2 2s2 222 22 sets; 22 seas; 2 sons; 2 men
 9   222 suns 22 subs 222 sins 22 saps 222 saws 22 sips 222 sirs
10   He got 22 pens, 22 pads, 22 pencils, and 22 clips on May 2.
11   The 22 seats in Row 22 were sold to 22 coeds from Room 222.
```

Keep the Sem finger in home-row position.

Use the L finger.

D. THE 9 KEY

```
12   lll lol l9l l9l 9l9 9l9 999 9 laws; 99 lots; 9 lies; 9 laps
13   99 labs 9 keys 9,992 kits 299 leis 999 legs 99 logs 29 lips
14   She moved from 929 29th Street to 922 92nd Avenue on May 9.
15   On May 9, the 99 men and 29 women baked 9 pies and 9 cakes.
```

Skillbuilding

E. NEW-KEY REVIEW

```
16  29-22 majority; 99-92 lead at half-time; 929 one-way roads;
17  92 cave-ins; 99 walk-ins; 92 up-to-date items; 22 tune-ups;
18  299 sign-ups; 929 fill-in-the-blank questions; 99 push-ups;
19  929 look-alikes; 922 go-getters; 29 T-shirts; 292 boo-boos;
```

F. PROGRESSIVE PRACTICE: ALPHABET

Follow the GDP software directions for this exercise to improve keystroking accuracy.

G. TECHNIQUE PRACTICE: HYPHEN

Make a dash by typing two hyphens with no space before, between, or after (lines 21 and 24). Note: Microsoft Word (but not the GDP software) automatically converts two hyphens into a formatted dash (—).

```
20      Larry will go to the next tennis tournament. I am
21  positive that he--like Lane--will find the event to be a
22  first-class sports event. If he can go, I will get all of
23  us first-rate seats.
24      Larry--but not Ella--enjoys going to tournaments that
25  are always first-rate, first-class sporting events.
```

H. 12-SECOND SPEED SPRINTS

Take three 12-second timed writings on each line. The scale below the last line shows your wpm speed for a 12-second timed writing.

```
26  Jan owns a pair of old gowns and a new hat she got from me.
27  He may go with us to the giant dock down by the handy lake.
28  His civic goal for the city is for them to endow the chair.
29  I may make us one set of maps to aid us when we visit them.
    ' ' ' '5' ' '10' ' '15' ' '20' ' '25' ' '30' ' '35' ' '40' ' '45' ' '50' ' '55' ' '60
```

I. 2-MINUTE TIMED WRITING

Take two 2-minute timed writings.

 **Goal:** At least 19wpm/2'/5e

```
30      Zachary just paid for six seats and quit because he      11
31  could not get the views he required near the middle of the   22
32  field. In August he thinks he may go to the ticket office    34
33  to purchase tickets.                                         38
    1 | 2 | 3 | 4 | 5 | 6 | 7 | 8 | 9 | 10 | 11 | 12
```

Enrichment • Lesson 11

Type each line 2 times.

A. NEW-KEY REINFORCEMENT

1 29-92 99-22 92-29 22-99 99-92 22-92 22-29 29-99 22-92 99-29
2 99-29 29-92 92-29 22-99 99-22 99-92 22-92 29-99 22-92 22-29
3 99-22 29-92 99-92 22-92 92-29 22-99 22-92 99-29 22-29 29-99

4 99 also-rans; 29 set-asides; 92 cure-alls; 29 two-by-fours;
5 92 free-for-alls; 29 do-it-yourselfers; 22 merry-go-rounds;
6 292 look-alikes; 929 flip-flops; 292 I-beams; 922 A-frames;

7 She had 92 pens, 29 pads, 99 pencils, 29 clips and 2 notes.
8 To dry-clean the 92 suits, use the 229 high-pressure hoses.
9 Only 22 off-the-record comments were heard from 292 people.

10 The 29 high-ranking men had to attend 22 black-tie affairs.
11 Over 99 part-time jobs were posted at the all-day job fair.
12 Use a 92-29 ratio in the 9-liter container on September 29.

B. ROW PRACTICE

Type each line 2 times.

Top Row

13 uproot Peter treetop typewriter witty purity quieter tiptoe
14 equity Europe prettier teeter quitter troop tutor write wee

Home Row

15 Dallas salads flask gassed ladled leash saddle shall shakes
16 slash ladles flakes flesh safes Allah salsa faked jags fall

Bottom row

17 Amman anemic annexing numb Venice menace examine Mexico ebb
18 Nancy convey become combat machine convene inn Manchu comma

C. PARAGRAPH TYPING

Type each paragraph 2 times.

19   This note is just to confirm my order on the basis of 11
20 the prices you quoted me on the phone. Let me know when you 23
21 ship five dozen boxes of staples for my light-duty machine. 35

22   Yes, I will be quite pleased to have you see the house 11
23 next week on Wednesday, if convenient. I feel sure you will 23
24 think it is just as great a prize as your main residence.   34

25   If we are to have an exciting project of any real size 11
26 this year, we need a more vigorous chair for it, so I will   23
27 request that you serve. I hope that will be okay with you.   35

    1 | 2 | 3 | 4 | 5 | 6 | 7 | 8 | 9 | 10 | 11 | 12

New Keys

Goals

- Touch-type the 8, 5, and ' keys.
- Type at least 20wpm/2'/5e.

A. WARMUP

alphabet | 1 | Dr. Jekyll vowed to finish zapping the quixotic bumblebees.
one hand | 2 | secret hominy dew hip beasts nonunion edge monk staff nylon
easy | 3 | Pamela may use a kayak and map to come to the old city dam.

New Keys

Use the K finger.

B. THE 8 KEY

4 kkk kik k8k k8k 8k8 8k8 888 88 kits; 88 kegs; 8 kin; 8 keys
5 828 kites 982 kings 828 kids 988 kilts 828 knees 998 knocks
6 On July 28, I saw 88 cats, 82 dogs, 88 birds, and 28 foxes.
7 Of the 828 people, 28 were at the free-for-all on April 28.

Use the F finger.

C. THE 5 KEY

8 fff frf f5f f5f 5f5 5f5 555 5 fans; 5 fibs; 5 figs; 58 firs
9 5 figs 5 foes 5 tins 5 taps 55 tons 58 bays 85 bids 95 boys
10 Just call me at 585-555-5955 or on my cell at 585-555-5585.
11 The 585 men, 952 women, and 852 children left on August 25.

Use the Sem finger.

D. THE ' KEY

12 ;;; ;'; ;'; ';' ';' ''' he'd; I've; Al's; it's; she's; I'll
13 all's can't cont'd dep't gov't we'll you're I'll lad's we'd
14 It's too bad that he'd eaten Kate's dessert at Abe's Diner.
15 I'm sure he won't mind if Joe's car isn't in Alan's garage.

Skillbuilding

E. NEW-KEY REVIEW

16 Li's 85-58 lead; Moe's and Bob's 82 ads; I'll take 59 bids;
17 Bob's sister can't type 85 wpm; 8585 East 85th Lane; 89-58;
18 pages 558-582; call her at 858-555-8958; 558 part-time ads;
19 Invoice 88-595; Apt. 58-B; I'll be in Room 588-D; May 5-28;

F. SUSTAINED PRACTICE: CAPITALS

Take a 1-minute timed writing on the boxed paragraph to establish your base speed. Then take a 1-minute timed writing on the following paragraph. As soon as you equal or exceed your base speed on this paragraph, move to the next, more difficult paragraph.

20   Even though he was only about thirty years old, Jason   11
21 knew that it was not too soon to begin thinking about his   23
22 retirement. He learned that many things were involved.   33

23   Even without considering the uncertainty of social   10
24 security, Jason knew that he should plan his career moves,   22
25 so he opened a new Individual Retirement Account in May.   34

26   When he became aware that The Longman Company would   11
27 match his contributions, Jason asked the Payroll Department   23
28 to open a retirement account for him with the Coplin Group.   34

29   He also learned that The Longman Company retirement   11
30 plan and his Individual Retirement Plan are all deferred   22
31 savings. Then, Jason purchased New Venture Group mutuals.   33

   1 | 2 | 3 | 4 | 5 | 6 | 7 | 8 | 9 | 10 | 11 | 12

G. 2-MINUTE TIMED WRITING

Take two 2-minute timed writings.

 **Goal:** At least 20wpm/2'/5e

32   Jack and Alex ordered six pizzas at a price that was   11
33 quite a bit lower than was the one they ordered yesterday.   23
34 They will order from the same place tomorrow for the party   34
35 they are wanting to provide.   40

   1 | 2 | 3 | 4 | 5 | 6 | 7 | 8 | 9 | 10 | 11 | 12

Enrichment • Lesson 12

Type each line 2 times.

A. NEW-KEY REINFORCEMENT

1 Mary's pages 58-85; John's 2,585 sales; 8858 O'Hara Street;
2 Call me at 858-555-8258; I'm in Room 859-B; Al's 58 errors;
3 cont'd on p. 285; 29,858 employees; 825 boys and 589 girls;

4 Pacers' final score of 89-82; May 28, '99; go to Room 2858;
5 Take I-85 to 92-B; Apt. 28-C; I'm 28.5 years old. He's out;
6 A tie score of 58-58; I'm out; the combination is 28-95-85;

Type each line 2 times.

B. ALPHABET PRACTICE

7 A Jack in the Box quickly varied its menu with fudge pizza.
8 Ban all foul toxic smog which can quickly jeopardize lives.
9 Five or six big jet planes zoomed quickly by the old tower.

10 Grumpy wizards made toxic brew for Jack and the evil queen.
11 If fog makes Max shiver, quickly zip down and buy a jacket.
12 Just keep examining every low bid quoted for zinc etchings.

13 Six crazy kings vowed to abolish my quite pitiful projects.
14 The jobs of waxing linoleum frequently peeved chintzy kids.
15 Weekly magazines request help for and by junior executives.

Type each paragraph 2 times.

C. PARAGRAPH TYPING

16   When I was at the gym today, I met Bill Saxon, the   10
17 former Jets quarterback. Bill is leaving football and needs 22
18 a job like the one we have open in hazardous control.   33

19   Folks do not want to live near airports because of   10
20 the extreme racket of the planes. The roar and whine as a   22
21 jet zooms by cannot be equaled by ten giant bulldozers.   33

22   If you accept this job, as we hope, please plan to   10
23 arrive next week so that we may zero in on those fashion   22
24 shows we have in Denver, Boston, Raleigh, and Quebec.   32

25   This is in response to your inquiry about Elizabeth 11
26 Jones. Ms. Jones worked for us for six years. We were sorry 23
27 to lose her to a company that gave her a larger salary.   34
    1 | 2 | 3 | 4 | 5 | 6 | 7 | 8 | 9 | 10 | 11 | 12

New Keys

13

Goals

- Touch-type the 4, 7, and : keys.
- Type at least 21wpm/2'/5e.

A. WARMUP

alphabet

1 Prized waxy jonquils choked the weeds in the big farm vats.

practice: *f* and *g*

2 gruff fig finger flag frogs gift golf gulf goofs fogs flags

easy

3 The new formal audit may be paid for by the downtown firms.

New Keys

Use the F finger.

B. THE 4 KEY

4 fff frf f4f f4f 4f4 4f4 444 4 fans; 4 fibs, 4 figs, 44 firs

5 4 figs 4 foes 4 tins 4 taps 44 tons 49 bays 45 bids 94 boys

6 The 44 men and 54 boys used 494 liters in 42 days on May 4.

7 Please add Items 428, 84, 944, 42, and 488 to Order 44-482.

Use the J finger.

C. THE 7 KEY

8 jjj juj j7j j7j 7j7 7j7 777 77 jugs; 7 jets; 7 jars; 7 jabs

9 74 jays 47 jobs 77 jots 74 hams 74 hats 47 hits 77 hugs 777

10 I bought Item 74 that weighs 47 pounds 7 ounces on June 27.

11 Allen covered pages 472-479, and Sue covered pages 277-789.

Use the Sem finger.

D. THE : KEY

The colon is the shift of the semicolon key. Do not space before or after a colon used with numbers. Space 1 time after a colon following a word except at the end of a line.

12 ;;; ;:; ;:; :;: :;: ::: 7:47 a.m.; 47:74 odds; Dear Mr. Ng:

13 Dr. Poole: Ms. Shu: Mr. Rose: Mrs. Tam: Dear Ed: Dear John:

14 Dear Johnny: Let's meet at 2:45 to discuss the 57:47 ratio.

15 Do not forget the Date:, To:, From:, and Subject: headings.

Skillbuilding

E. NEW-KEY REVIEW

```
16  The 47 managers had 74 tickets for the 4:47 game on May 24.
17  as follows: these people: this motion: here it is: Dear Jo:
18  Ed's 97-42 lead at 4:25 p.m.; pages 477-747; a 747 jet; Hi:
```

PPP   PRETEST » PRACTICE » POSTTEST

PRETEST
Take a 1-minute timed writing.

F. PRETEST: Common Letter Combinations

```
19      The condo committee was hoping the motion would not be    11
20  forced upon it, realizing that viable solutions ought to be   23
21  developed. It was forceful in seeking a period of time.       34
        1 | 2 | 3 | 4 | 5 | 6 | 7 | 8 | 9 | 10 | 11 | 12
```

PRACTICE
Speed Emphasis:
If you made 2 or fewer errors on the Pretest, type each *individual* line 2 times.
Accuracy Emphasis:
If you made 3 or more errors, type each *group* of lines (as though it were a paragraph) 2 times.

G. PRACTICE: Word Beginnings

```
22  for forum forge forced forgot formal forest foreign forerun
23  con conks conic consul confer convey convex contact concern
24  per perks peril person period perish permit percale percent
```

H. PRACTICE: Word Endings

```
25  ing tying hiking liking edging bowing hoping having nursing
26  ble fable pebble treble tumble viable dabble fumble fusible
27  ion union legion nation region motion potion option bastion
```

POSTTEST
Repeat the Pretest timed writing and compare performance.

Take two 2-minute timed writings.

 **Goal:** At least 21wpm/2'/5e

I. POSTTEST: Common Letter Combinations

J. 2-MINUTE TIMED WRITING

```
28      Jim told Bev that they must keep the liquid oxygen      10
29  frozen so that it could be used by the new plant managers   22
30  tomorrow. The oxygen will then be moved quickly to its new  34
31  location by transport or rail on Tuesday.                   42
        1 | 2 | 3 | 4 | 5 | 6 | 7 | 8 | 9 | 10 | 11 | 12
```

Enrichment • Lesson 13

Type each line 2 times.

A. NEW-KEY REINFORCEMENT

1 Jill bought 29 tickets for the 8:25 or 7:45 show on July 5.
2 Maxine called from 777-555-4278 or 777-555-4279 for Martin.
3 Jackson sold 85 tires, 94 air filters, and 247 oil filters.

4 Flight 4789B departed at 8:45 a.m. and arrived at 9:25 p.m.
5 I'm moving from 4529 East Rogers to 4725 East Eaton in May.
6 Only 247 men and 74 women attended the orientation at 8:45.

7 Ty: Flight 982 on the 747 jet departs at 2:45 on August 27.
8 On November 24-27, we were open from 7:45 a.m. to 9:45 p.m.
9 The 89 men then drove 774 miles on Route 47-B and Route 77.

Type each line 2 times.

B. SUBSTITUTION ERRORS

10 r-t hurt trot trite Trent treat tutor tort trust rotate try
11 m-n mend mine norm unman many naming morn manual hymn amend
12 o-i void silo olio Ohio into icon coin polio folio boil oil

13 a-s tasks visas sodas seams scans areas bases sales say has
14 s-d suds soda sides sheds dusts dudes dosed desks deeds sad
15 r-e rear refer every erred enter emery elder Erie eerie red

16 v-b visible brave bovine vibe livable above bevy bevel verb
17 w-e endow wade wee ewe wide dew wed elbow we where were wet
18 f-g flags fogs gruff goof gulf golf gift frog flag fang fig

Type each paragraph 2 times.

C. PARAGRAPH TYPING

19   The senator quietly voted to legalize marijuana but   11
20 drew the line at making it easily available to teens. He   22
21 also voted for new price controls on all foreign exports.   33

22   The anxious job applicant inquired about the size of   11
23 the firm's overseas business. He also wanted to know the   22
24 weekly sales of gas and other petroleum products to China.   34

25   I jotted down all the questions I wanted to ask the   11
26 five energy czars the next time I met with them. They were   23
27 in town for the big expo being held at the city arena.   33

28   Three weekly magazines requested help for the junior   11
29 executives in the software industry. By now, they must have   23
30 received many responses from their readers and subscribers.   35

       1 | 2 | 3 | 4 | 5 | 6 | 7 | 8 | 9 | 10 | 11 | 12

New Keys

14

Goals

- Touch-type the 6, 3, and / keys.
- Type at least 22wpm/2′/5e.

A. WARMUP

alphabet	1	Max did not become eloquent over a zany gift like jodhpurs.
frequent digraphs	2	te tee ate byte tell tea termite ten Ute tent teed teen Ted
easy	3	The auditor's panel had the right to risk a firm's profits.

New Keys

Use the J finger.

B. THE ⬛ KEY

4   jjj jyj j6j j6j 6j6 6j6 666 66 jugs; 6 jets; 6 jars; 6 jabs
5   64 jays 46 jobs 66 jots 67 hams 76 hats 46 hits 67 hugs 666
6   Tom Quin left at 6:26 p.m. on Train 66 to travel 626 miles.
7   There were 56,646 people in Bath and 26,269 in Hale in May.

Use the D finger.

C. THE ⬛ KEY

8   ddd ded d3d d3d 3d3 3d3 333 33 dots; 3 dies; 3 dips; 3 days
9   332 days 36 dogs 63 does 73 duds 37 dies 3:39 p.m.; 323-373
10   The 33 vans moved 36 cases in less than 33 hours on July 3.
11   Please add 55 to 753 and subtract 73 to get a total of 735.

Use the Sem finger.

D. THE ⬛ KEY

Do not space before or after the slash—unless it is the last character of an expression (line 15).

12   ;;; ;/; ;/; /;/ /;/ /// a/an and/or at/about bad/badly I/me
13   both/each disc/disk farther/further fewer/less like/such as
14   On 6/2/99, you asked him/her if he/she selected true/false.
15   Visit http://gdpkeyboarding.com/ for any questions/answers.

Skillbuilding

E. NEW-KEY REVIEW: 6, 3, AND SLASH KEY

16 In 6 months, he had walked 36 miles and/or driven 63 miles.
17 I realize that 3/6 of the 66 shipments equals 33 shipments.
18 He was born in New York on 6/3/36 and died there on 6/6/63.
19 Lucille bought 36 his/her towels on 3/3 with terms of n/29.

F. NUMBER-KEY REVIEW: 2, 4, 5, 7, 8, AND 9

20 My staff of 24 worked a total of 87 hours on Project 598-B.
21 Ed's instructor assigned pages 549-782 to be read by May 2.
22 From 2:45 p.m. until 5:45 p.m., I'll be typing in Room 987.
23 Let's visit her at 592 North Elm, Apt. 47, on September 28.

G. TECHNIQUE PRACTICE: SHIFT KEY

Type each line 2 times. After striking the capitalized letter, return the SHIFT key finger immediately to home-row position.

24 Alex Bly and Clara Dye wed. Ella Fochs and Gil Hall talked.
25 Ida Jackson met Kay Lang for a fast lunch at Mamma Nancy's.
26 Otis Pike should call Quint Richards about Sophia Townsend.
27 Ulrich Volte will take Winona Xi to visit Yadkin in Zurich.

H. PROGRESSIVE PRACTICE: ALPHABET

Follow the GDP software directions for this exercise to improve keystroking speed.

I. 2-MINUTE TIMED WRITING

Take two 2-minute timed writings.

Goal: At least 22wpm/2'/5e

28   Jack scheduled a science quiz next week for Gregory,   11
29 but he did not let him know what time the exam was to be   22
30 taken. Gregory must score well on the exam in order to be   34
31 admitted to the class at the private Mount Academy.   44

    1 | 2 | 3 | 4 | 5 | 6 | 7 | 8 | 9 | 10 | 11 | 12

Enrichment • Lesson 14

Type each line 2 times.

A. NUMBER-KEY REINFORCEMENT

1 The 375 cars traveled 847 miles and used 45 gallons of gas.
2 My staff of 24 worked 48 hours a week from May 6 to May 29.
3 The 6 teams comprised 69 girls and 7 boys and left at 9:45.

4 The 37 men visited the 45 women at 3:25 p.m. on October 26.
5 Larry's 29 basketball players scored 467 points on 6/23/99.
6 The 23 workers packed 87 cartons, which weighed 389 pounds.

Type each line 2 times. Type the 3-letter word, backspace, and type the new letter. Thus, *rat* becomes *ram*.

B. TECHNIQUE PRACTICE: BACKSPACE KEY

7   rat←m gut←m are←m tip←n rut←n pat←n gut←n did←n bit←n ale←l
8   ash←k woo←k pat←l cot←n fit←n mat←n put←n tap←n wit←n ton←o
9   elk←m ill←k air←l bat←n fur←n owe←n rat←n air←m get←m sin←p
10 inn←k ire←k ilk←l but←n dot←n ink←n pet←n hat←m hit←m air←l

Take three 12-second timed writings on each line. The scale below the last line shows your wpm speed for a 12-second timed writing.

C. 12-SECOND SPEED SPRINTS

11 The doe and buck by the old lake may dig up the giant oaks.
12 It is a shame she works such an odd bowl into her art work.
13 Jake moved to amend the law to let the worker take the job.
14 He may sign over the title to his autos when he is in town.
```
' ' ' '5' ' ' '10' ' ' '15' ' '20' ' ' '25' ' ' '30' ' ' '35' ' ' '40' ' ' '45' ' ' '50' ' ' '55' ' ' '60
```

Type each paragraph 2 times.

D. PARAGRAPH TYPING

15   My boss knew that her expert eloquence was just a big   11
16 hazard to effective teamwork, so he asked her to tone down 23
17 her remarks when giving her opinions on our progress.   33

18   Six of the female employees quietly gave back their   11
19 prizes to the judge because they did not agree with his   22
20 decisions regarding the basis for making his decisions.   33

21   Please, just be very quick and careful when you fix   11
22 the size of the tables in your annual report. You should   22
23 get Margaret to help you proofread your final report.   33

24   Our firm should ban all foul toxic smog because it   10
25 can quickly jeopardize the lives of our workers and their   22
26 families. I hope the board will make this decision soon.   33
```
 1 | 2 | 3 | 4 | 5 | 6 | 7 | 8 | 9 | 10 | 11 | 12
```

Review

15

Goals

• Type at least 23wpm/2′/5e.

A. WARMUP

alphabet 1 Jack amazed a few girls by dropping the antique onyx vases.
alternate-hand words 2 half height right penalty with visit social lens rigid snap
easy 3 My mangy dog then ran to his bowl in the den to take a sip.

Skillbuilding

B. NUMBER-KEY REVIEW

4 I sent 72 jars, 89 cans, 29 boxes, and 32 bags to 33 homes.
5 The 494 students partied at 576 Dale and then at 5896 Park.
6 We got seats 27, 25, 28, 67, and 79 for the August 98 game.

7 Open Rooms 325, 343, 467, and 456 with Master Key No. 65-7.
8 The equipment shed was 267 by 278 feet, not 289 by 93 feet.
9 Mail the 378 packages to 548 East 65th Lane, not to 46 Elm.

C. PUNCTUATION REVIEW

. 10 Go to Reno. Drive to Yuma. Call Mary. Get Samuel. See Cory.
, 11 We saw Nice, Paris, Bern, Rome, Munich, Bonn, and Shanghai.
; 12 Type the memo; read my report; get pens; get paper; see me.

:- 13 Dear Aldo: Read these pages by 9:45: 2-9, 26-35, and 45-78.
' 14 Ted's car and Ann's truck took the Hills' kids to Shoney's.
/ 15 My aunt/best friend was born on 6/22/37 and died on 9/2/95.

D. PROGRESSIVE PRACTICE: ALPHABET

Follow the GDP software directions for this exercise to improve keystroking accuracy.

E. TECHNIQUE PRACTICE: TAB KEY

Press TAB where you see the ➜ symbol.

```
16  Kim➜ apt➜ Mac➜ art➜ Nat➜ Meg➜ ads➜ arm➜ all➜ ado➜ Joy
17  Orr➜ awl➜ Jan➜ Ida➜ Moe➜ Lin➜ zap➜ Joe➜ zed➜ ark➜ awe
18  Kai➜ Lev➜ add➜ ask➜ Mom➜ Uri➜ Jeb➜ Nan➜ aid➜ Lot➜ amp
19  Jay➜ Hal➜ Ima➜ Ira➜ ail➜ aim➜ Ian➜ Max➜ Pat➜ Liv➜ Jim
```

F. TECHNIQUE PRACTICE: SPACE BAR

```
20  A toy dog in the pen is apt to be a big hit at the new gym.
21  We may go to the zoo for the day if the sun is not too hot.
22  Eli and Max may use a map to see how to get to the new pub.
23  If it is to be, it is up to you and Ben to do it for a fee.
```

G. 2-MINUTE TIMED WRITING

Take two 2-minute timed writings.

 Goal: At least 23wpm/2'/5e

```
24        Jeff Melvin was quite busy fixing all of the frozen    11
25  pipes so that his water supply would not be stopped. Last    22
26  winter Jeff kept the pipes from freezing by wrapping them    34
27  with an insulated tape that protected them from snow and     45
28  ice.                                                          46
        1 |  2 |  3 |  4 |  5 |  6 |  7 |  8 |  9 | 10 | 11 | 12
```

Enrichment • Lesson 15

Type each line 2 times.

A. NUMBER-KEY REINFORCEMENT

1 Just call me at 275-555-8346 or on my cell at 748-555-9292.
2 I bought Item 536 that weighs 45 pounds 6 ounces on May 27.
3 She moved from 859 36th Street to 734 82nd Avenue on May 5.

4 On July 26, I saw 67 cats, 92 dogs, 83 birds, and 49 foxes.
5 Please add Items 526, 73, 989, 24, and 453 to Order 56-627.
6 The 587 police met at 2:25 a.m. with 89 agents in Room 324.

Type each line 2 times.

B. ALPHABET PRACTICE

7 A campus TV quiz just asks why gold is buried at Fort Knox.
8 Crazy Fredrick bought Jane many very exquisite opal jewels.
9 All questions asked by five watch experts amazed the judge.

10 Jack quietly gave the dog owners most of his prized boxers.
11 Fred specialized in the job of making very quaint wax toys.
12 Six big devils from Japan then quickly forgot how to waltz.

Take three 12-second timed writings on each line. The scale below the last line shows your wpm speed for a 12-second timed writing.

C. 12-SECOND SPEED SPRINTS

13 He may go with us to the giant dock down by the handy lake.
14 The doe and buck by the old bush may dig up the giant oaks.
15 Ken had a dish of lamb and cut up a mango and a ripe mango.
16 Kay may visit the big island in May when she is down there.
   ' ' ' '5' ' ' '10' ' ' '15' ' ' '20' ' ' '25' ' ' '30' ' ' '35' ' ' '40' ' ' '45' ' ' '50' ' ' '55' ' ' '60

Type each paragraph 2 times.

D. PARAGRAPH TYPING

17   Please ship to me by freight sixty dozen quart jars   11
18 and twelve dozen black pans for the opening of our newest   22
19 appliance store in the coming weeks in North Carolina.   33

20   Mr. Dave Jones, the defense attorney, quickly spotted   11
21 four women dozing in the jury box. He moved to have the   22
22 judge quickly declare a mistrial and dismiss the jurors.   33

23   Back in June, our company delivered oxygen equipment   11
24 of odd sizes to the county hospital. It has already been   22
25 installed and is working properly in the emergency room.   33

26   I saw the four brown foxes who were quickly jumping   11
27 over the lazy dogs that were resting out back. The dogs did 23
28 not even open their eyes but continued sleeping heavily.   34
    1 | 2 | 3 | 4 | 5 | 6 | 7 | 8 | 9 | 10 | 11 | 12

Keyboarding: Numbers and Symbols

New Keys

16

Goals

- Touch-type the &, $, and 0 keys.
- Type at least 24wpm/2′/5e.

A. WARMUP

alphabet 1 Jack's man found exactly a quarter in the woven zipper bag.
concentration 2 oversimplifications nonrepresentational professionalization
easy 3 An auditor may sign a form that may name Toby to the panel.

New Keys

Use the J
finger.

B. THE & KEY

The ampersand key (the sign for *and*) is the shift of 7. In normal narrative writing, space 1 time before and after the ampersand.

4 jjj juj j&j j&j &j& &j& &&& Max & Dee & Sue & Tom & Rex & I
5 Brown & Sons shipped to May & Lee and also to Dye & Pearce.
6 John & Loo brought a case against May & Green and Li & Won.
7 Von & Trapp and Den & Sax were joined by Contreras & Duran.

Use the F
finger.

C. THE $ KEY

The dollar sign is the shift of 4. Do not space between the dollar sign and the following number.

8 fff frf f$f f$f f f $$$ $44 $434.44 $4,444 $456 $492.85
9 He paid $48, $64, and $94 for the chairs plus $48 shipping.
10 Last season's concert tickets were $35, $45, $75, and $255.
11 If you add $48.62, $49.93, and $324.42, you'll get $422.97.

Keep the J finger in home-row position.

Use the Sem finger.

D. THE 0 KEY

12 ;;; ;p; ;0; ;0; 0;0 0;0 000 00 2:00; 3:00; 4:00; 5:00; 6:30
13 The 80 men met at 3:05 with 20 agents in Room 90 on May 20.
14 I paid $40.05 for 20 pens and $50.50 for 30 pads on May 30.
15 The firm of Mori & Itou at 200 Broad Street owes us $8,000.

Skillbuilding

E. NEW-KEY REVIEW

16 $20.50 & $380.65 & $90.20 & $40.50 & $30.40 & $247.50 & $80
17 We hired Rizzo & Kelly for $20,000 to help Diamond & Green.
18 Arn & Sons owed us $4,000 and paid us only $250.50 in July.
19 Call Penn & Ames at 800-555-2040 and ask about the $48,000.

F. PACED PRACTICE

Follow the GDP software directions for this exercise to improve keystroking speed and accuracy.

G. TECHNIQUE PRACTICE: SHIFT KEY

20 Ann Bonn asked for lunch. Colin Dix and Elaine Fochs moved.
21 Glen Hans filed as Iris James typed. Les Kay talked loudly.
22 Maya Nevins and Orin Parks tried. Quinn Roberts lost a bet.
23 Skye Tynch sat. Uriah Vin and Winn Xung ate. Yosef Zoe hid.

H. PROGRESSIVE PRACTICE: ALPHABET

Follow the GDP software directions for this exercise to improve keystroking speed.

Take two 2-minute timed writings.

Goal: At least 24wpm/2'/5e

I. 2-MINUTE TIMED WRITING

24   Ginny quit her zoo job seven days after she learned   11
25 that she was expected to travel to four zoos in the first   22
26 month of work. After she had quit her job, she found an   34
27 excellent position that did not require her to be away   48
28 from home so much.

    1 | 2 | 3 | 4 | 5 | 6 | 7 | 8 | 9 | 10 | 11 | 12

Enrichment • Lesson 16

Type each line 2 times.

A. NEW-KEY REVIEW

1 Ali & Wu; Ash & Li; Cho & Ng; Day & Ivy; Gil & Ray; Ho & Yu
2 $234.56 and $78.54 and $463.38 and $23,896.25 and $4,993.39
3 20 and 30 and 40 and 50 and 60 and 70 and 80 and 90 and 200
4 Ott & Orr owed $5,000 to me; they owed $7,000 to Jay & Poe.

B. SUSTAINED PRACTICE: SYLLABIC INTENSITY

Syllabic intensity refers to the average number of syllables per word in a passage. The higher the syllabic intensity, the more difficult the passage is to type.

Take a 1-minute timed writing on the boxed paragraph to establish your base speed. Then take a 1-minute timed writing on the following paragraph. As soon as you equal or exceed your base speed on this paragraph, move to the next, more difficult paragraph.

5   One should always attempt to maintain good health. As   11
6 the first step in keeping good health, one should avoid the   23
7 habit of smoking. Volumes have been written on this topic.   35

8   A second habit that will help maintain your health for   11
9 decades is consuming an appropriate amount of water, day in   23
10 and day out. Most doctors recommend eight glasses a day.   34

11   Making exercise a habit is another important trait for   11
12 staying in good health. Most experts agree that spending a   23
13 few minutes a day in regular, vigorous exercise is helpful.   35

14   A final habit of importance is maintaining appropriate   11
15 body weight. The key to maintaining weight is developing a   23
16 positive eating pattern. Calculating calories is helpful.   34

        1 | 2 | 3 | 4 | 5 | 6 | 7 | 8 | 9 | 10 | 11 | 12

C. PARAGRAPH TYPING

Type each paragraph 2 times.

17   Jack typed a requisition for white moving boxes of   10
18 various sizes--some long and some short. He will need them   22
19 when we move into our new headquarters sometime next month.   34

20   My grandfather picked up a quartz and onyx necklace   11
21 for my grandmother at the bazaar. He knew that she loved   22
22 jewelry, and he was eager to give it to her on Christmas.   33

23   Jeff had his size, which helped him quickly win over   11
24 Gene in the boxing match. He won based on both his size and   23
25 his abilities as a boxer. My school was quite proud of him.   35

        1 | 2 | 3 | 4 | 5 | 6 | 7 | 8 | 9 | 10 | 11 | 12

New Keys

Goals

- Touch-type the 1, ?, and @ keys.
- Type at least 25wpm/2'/5e.

A. WARMUP

alphabet	1	Many big jackdaws quickly zipped over those empty fox pens.
one hand	2	street unholy sad you stated monopoly seat pink treat unpin
easy	3	Duane may try to fix the auditory problems in the city gym.

New Keys

Keep the F finger in home-row position.

Use the A finger.

B. THE 1 KEY

4 aaa aqa a1a a1a 1a1 1a1 111 11 ants; 11 asps; 1 aim; 11 ads
5 Sam left here at 1:11, Susan at 6:11, and Don at 11:11 a.m.
6 Erich had moved from 1010 Main Street to 1101 Main in 1990.
7 Sarah left at 11:00 a.m. on Train No. 11 to go 1,100 miles.

Use the Sem finger.

C. THE ? KEY

The question mark is the shift of the slash. Space 1 time after a question mark.

8 ;;; ;/; ;?; ;?; ?;? ?;? ??? Who? What? When? Where? Why me?
9 May I? Why not? Who called? Need a job? Which one? Is it I?
10 Who's there? Any questions? Yes? Need some help? Who cares?
11 Is it 11:00? Was it held on 11/11/09? Where is 1101 W. Elm?

Use the S finger.

D. THE @ KEY

The at sign is the shift of 2. Space 1 time before and after the at sign except when it is used in an e-mail address (lines 13 and 15).

12 sss sws s@s s@s @s@ @s@ @@@ Buy 15 @ $41.01 and 11 @ $3.15.
13 E-mail me at jfox@tmu.edu or at jfox01@aol.com on April 11.
14 Order 12 pens @ $14, 185 pads @ $16, and 110 clips @ $2.50.
15 Can you e-mail Roger at rlowe@umn.edu to order 250 @ $1.15?

Skillbuilding

E. NEW-KEY REVIEW

16 Who knows if Randy's e-mail address is rjoyner@hotmail.com?
17 Should she buy 150 shares @ $11.50 and 200 shares @ $11.25?
18 Did she change her e-mail address to dcberkow011@yahoo.com?
19 Did Beverly try cokeefe011@vmu.edu or caroleoke101@msn.com?

F. TECHNIQUE PRACTICE: BACKSPACE KEY

Directions: Type the 3-letter word, backspace, and type the new letter.

20 bud←m gig←n dew←n rag←m tad←n own←l get←m tie←n toe←n
21 car←p hoe←g yea←n pie←n vat←n hug←m rug←m pod←i per←p
22 job←y yaw←m bus←y pad←l lad←p the←y nag←p fur←n nub←n
23 fad←n max←y jag←m fig←n ice←y oaf←k add←o mow←p log←o

G. MAP+: ALPHABET

Follow the GDP software directions for this exercise to improve keystroking accuracy.

H. 2-MINUTE TIMED WRITING

Take two 2-minute timed writings.

Goal: At least 25wpm/2'/5e

24   From the tower John saw that those six big planes   11
25 could crash as they zoomed quickly over treetops on their   22
26 way to the demonstration that was scheduled to begin very   33
27 soon. We hope there are no accidents and that the pilots   45
28 reach the airport quickly.   50
       1 | 2 | 3 | 4 | 5 | 6 | 7 | 8 | 9 | 10 | 11 | 12

Enrichment • Lesson 17

Type each line 2 times.

1
?
@
1 ? @

A. NEW-KEY REINFORCEMENT

1 Adam moved from 1101 Oak Lane to 2110 11th Street on May 1.
2 Who knows? Does Karina? Cloris? Gamal? How about Salvatore?
3 Order 328 @ $4.50 and 390 @ $16.75 from renees@comcast.net.
4 Whose address is luan111@msn.com? Whose is wells101@cc.com?

Type each line 2 times.

B. NUMBER PRACTICE

5 we 23 ere 343 wry 246 woe 293 ask 128 lay 916 did 383 to 59
6 err 344 I 8 it 85 quit 1785 pup 070 pre 043 rip 480 tie 583
7 yew 632 quip 1780 ow 92 ire 843 per 034 pry 046 is 82 do 39

PPP

PRETEST » PRACTICE » POSTTEST

PRETEST
Take a 1-minute timed writing.

PRACTICE
Speed Emphasis:
If you made no more than 2 errors on the Pretest, type each *individual* line 2 times.
Accuracy Emphasis:
If you made 3 or more errors, type each *group* of lines (as though it were a paragraph) 2 times.

POSTTEST
Repeat the Pretest timed writing and compare performance.

C. PRETEST: Close Reaches

8   Casey hoped that we were not wasting good grub. After   11
9 the sun went down, he swiftly put the oleo and plums in the 23
10 cart. Bart opened a copy of an old book; Grant had a swim. 35
    1 | 2 | 3 | 4 | 5 | 6 | 7 | 8 | 9 | 10 | 11 | 12

D. PRACTICE: Adjacent Keys

11 op hope flop open mops rope opera droop scope copier trophy
12 we west owed went weld weep weigh weary wedge wealth plowed
13 rt hurt port cart dirt fort court party start hearty parted

E. PRACTICE: Consecutive Fingers

14 un tune spun unit dune punt under prune sunny hunter uneasy
15 gr grow grim grab grub grew great graze gripe greasy grassy
16 ol role oleo pool sold hole troll folly polka stolen oldest

F. POSTTEST: Close Reaches

New Keys

18

Goals

- Touch-type the % ( ) and # keys.
- Type at least 26wpm/2'/5e.

A. WARMUP

alphabet
1 My woven silk pajamas can be exchanged for the blue quartz.

practice: *s* and *d*
2 ads sad deeds desks dosed dudes dusts sheds sides soda suds

easy
3 Her ruby handiwork is fine, and she is so proficient at it.

New Keys

Use the F finger.

B. THE [%] KEY

Percent is the shift of 5. Do not space between the number and the percent sign.

4 fff frf f%f f%f %f% %f% %%% 10% 9% 8% 7% 6% 5% 4% 3% 2% 10%
5 Rob quoted rates of 8%, 9%, 10%, 11%, and 12% on the bonds.
6 Sandy scored 82%, Jan 89%, Ken 90%, and me 91% on the exam.
7 Only 55% scored 75% or higher, and 8% scored 90% or higher.

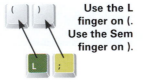

**Use the L finger on (.
Use the Sem finger on).**

C. THE [(] AND [)] KEYS

Parentheses are the shifts of 9 and 0. Do not space between the parentheses and the text within them.

8 lll lol l(l l(l (l((l((((;;; ;p; ;); ;););));)))) (a)
9 Please ask (1) Al, (2) Pat, (3) Ted, (4) Dee, and (5) Lise.
10 He'll (a) take two aspirin, (b) go to bed, and (c) rest up.
11 Rosa's (a cafe) had fish (shad) on the menu today (Monday).

Use the D finger.

D. THE # KEY

The # sign stands for *number* if it comes before a figure and *pounds* if it comes after a figure. It is the shift of 3. Do not space between the # sign and the number.

```
12   ddd ded d#d d#d #d# #d# ### #3 #33 #333 33# 83#; 37# of #83
13   Write down 330# of #200 and 380# of #400 using a #2 pencil.
14   We sat in seats #12, #34, #56, #65, and #66 at the concert.
15   Please use 50# lined paper for #373 and 30# paper for #374.
```

Skillbuilding

E. NEW-KEY REVIEW

```
16   Policy 8(b) says to load Truck #48 with 2,000# of 50% sand.
17   We need 85# of #2 grade ore (aluminum) and 45# of #3 grade.
18   Nearly 60% of the males and 50% of the females chose #5738.
19   Just stress (a) speed 50% of the time and (b) accuracy 50%.
```

F. PROGRESSIVE PRACTICE: NUMBERS

Follow the GDP software directions for this exercise to improve keystroking speed.

G. TECHNIQUE PRACTICE: SPACE BAR

```
20   Eli and Max may use a map to see how to get to the new pub.
21   A toy dog in the pen is apt to be a big hit at the new gym.
22   If it is to be, it is up to you and Ben to do it for a fee.
23   We may go to the zoo for the day if the sun is not too hot.
```

Take two 2-minute timed writings.

Goal: At least 26wpm/2'/5e

H. 2-MINUTE TIMED WRITING

```
24        Max had to make one quick adjustment to his television   11
25   set before the football game began. The picture during the   23
26   last game was fuzzy and hard to see. If he cannot fix the     35
27   picture, he may have to purchase a new television set; and    46
28   that may be difficult to do.                                  52
       1 |  2 |  3 |  4 |  5 |  6 |  7 |  8 |  9 | 10 | 11 | 12
```

Enrichment • Lesson 18

Type each line 2 times.

%
( )
#
% ( ) #

Type each line 2 times.

A. NEW-KEY REINFORCEMENT

1 Of the 85% of the alumni here, 9% gave 28% and 6% gave 25%.
2 Just (a) stop, (b) look, and (c) listen to her (Iphigenia).
3 Please record 33# of #200 and 38# of #400 on the #20 paper.
4 Only 15% of them (the attendees) ordered 30# of item #5011.

B. NUMBER PRACTICE

5 we 23 ort 945 rep 430 pot 095 toy 596 yip 680 yow 692 it 85
6 tee 533 ore 943 weep 2330 pop 090 poi 098 top 590 quit 1785
7 quip 1780 tip 580 woo 299 try 546 out 975 pro 049 quay 1716

C. SUSTAINED PRACTICE: NUMBERS

Take a 1-minute timed writing on the boxed paragraph to establish your base speed. Then take a 1-minute timed writing on the following paragraph. As soon as you equal or exceed your base speed on this paragraph, move to the next, more difficult paragraph.

8   Michael learned through firsthand experience last week   11
9 that the cost of a week at the beach varies a great deal.   23
10 He says that a rowboat would be about right for his money. 34

11 His Uncle Bo told him that when he was his age, he had   11
12 rented a small cabin for the huge sum of $105 for one week. 23
13 For $23 more, he rented a small boat and outboard motor.   34

14 Then Uncle Bo went on to say that when he rented the   11
15 same cabin last year, the cost had gone up to either $395   22
16 or $410. Boat and motor rentals now cost from $62 to $87.   34

17 Aunt Kate said that she and her husband will be paying   11
18 either $1,946 or $2,073 for a week's sailing on the 53-foot 23
19 yacht. The boat has a 4-person crew and was built in 2006.   35

    1 | 2 | 3 | 4 | 5 | 6 | 7 | 8 | 9 | 10 | 11 | 12

D. PACED PRACTICE

Follow the GDP software directions for this exercise to improve keystroking speed and accuracy.

E. PARAGRAPH TYPING

Type each paragraph 2 times.

20 I saw five or six of the big jet planes zoom quickly   11
21 over an old tower by the side of the road. They were flying 23
22 in formation and created a beautiful display for everyone.   34

23 Brown jars of an acidic mixture prevented the solution 11
24 from freezing so quickly. It took about four days for it to 23
25 freeze solid; then we could store it in the lab's freezer.   35

    1 | 2 | 3 | 4 | 5 | 6 | 7 | 8 | 9 | 10 | 11 | 12

New Keys

Goals

- Touch-type the ” ! and * keys.
- Type at least 27wpm/2′/5e.

A. WARMUP

alphabet	1 The jinxed wizards plucked the ivy stem from the big quilt.
frequent digraphs	2 on bon con none noon don ion one son ton won onto moon font
easy	3 Jan and her son may make a bowl of fish and a cup of cocoa.

New Keys

 Use the Sem finger.

B. THE ” KEY

The quotation key is the shift of the apostrophe. Do not space between quotation marks and the text they enclose.

4   ;;; ;”; ;”; ”;” ”;” ”” “Thanks,” he said, “I needed that.”
5   I read her article, “Freaking Out,” and said, “It is great.”
6   “Those were wonderful,” Fidel said. “I’ll take seven more.”
7   Juan wanted to know if the name was “Roberto” or “Roberta.”

 Use the A finger.

C. THE ! KEY

The exclamation mark is the shift of 1. Space 1 time after an exclamation mark.

8   aaa aqa a!a a!a !a! !a! !!! Wow! Now! Go! Stay! Sit! Nurse!
9   Put it down! Do not move! Leave it there! Get out! Move it!
10   Ouch! That hurt! Let’s roll! Incredible! Hang in there! No!
11   Congratulations! That was great! Don’t shoot! Oh, no! Help!

Use the K finger.

D. THE ![*] KEY

The asterisk is the shift of 8. Do not space before the asterisk but space 1 time after the asterisk.

```
12  kkk kik k*k k*k *k* *k* *** p. 18* as follows:* Note* etc.*
13  An * may be used to indicate a footnote at the page bottom.
14  In the footnote itself, do not leave any space after the *.
15  Did he really call Mr. Baines a *****? Wow! That was awful!
```

Skillbuilding

E. NEW-KEY REVIEW

```
16  The right word* was "parenthesis" instead of "parentheses."
17  "Wow!" Aki said, "That* was an amazing display! Go see it."
18  "Only one* was allowed in," said Jin. "It was Mr. Mystery."
19  The source* was absolutely reliable! "I agree," Yaron said.
```

F. MAP+: NUMBERS

Follow the GDP software directions for this exercise to improve keystroking accuracy.

G. PLACEMENT OF QUOTATION MARKS

1. The closing quotation mark is always typed *after* a period or comma (line 20) but *before* a colon or semicolon (line 21).
2. The closing quotation mark is typed *after* a question mark or exclamation point if the quoted material itself is a question or an exclamation (line 22). Otherwise, the quotation mark is typed *before* the question mark or exclamation point (line 23).

```
20  "Hi, there," I said. "My name is Karen, and I am new here."
21  James said, "I'll mail the check tomorrow"; but he did not.
22  Raheem read the article "Will They Succeed on the Economy?"
23  Did Anne say, "We won"? I was shocked when Juan said, "Me"!
```

H. PACED PRACTICE

Follow the GDP software directions for this exercise to improve keystroking speed and accuracy.

I. TECHNIQUE PRACTICE: TAB KEY

Press TAB where you see the →.

```
24  Orr→ Ike→ zoo→ Jon→ apt→ Pat→ ado→ zap→ Ned→ asp→ zag
25  Jan→ Lev→ Kit→ Ida→ Joy→ ads→ Joe→ ago→ Ima→ are→ ace
26  Mac→ Jim→ ate→ Lou→ Mia→ zed→ add→ Pia→ Moe→ Lot→ Jay
27  zip→ Obi→ Mom→ aft→ Job→ age→ Ham→ Ott→ awl→ art→ Hsu
```

J. 2-MINUTE TIMED WRITING

Take two 2-minute timed writings.

 **Goal:** At least 27wpm/2'/5e

```
28      Topaz and onyx rings were for sale at very reasonable   11
29  prices last month. When Jeanette saw the rings with these   23
30  stones, she quickly bought them both for her sons. These    34
31  jewels were difficult to find, and Jeanette was pleased     45
32  she could purchase those rings when she did.                54
     1 | 2 | 3 | 4 | 5 | 6 | 7 | 8 | 9 | 10 | 11 | 12
```

Strategies for Career Success

Being a Good Listener

Silence is golden! Listening is essential for learning, getting along, and forming relationships.

Do you tend to forget people's names after being introduced? Do you look away from the speaker instead of making eye contact? Do you interrupt the speaker before he or she finishes talking? Do you misunderstand people? Answering yes can indicate poor listening skills.

To improve your listening skills, follow these steps. *Hear the speaker clearly.* Do not interrupt; let the speaker develop his or her ideas before you speak. *Focus on the message.* At the end of a conversation, identify major items discussed. Mentally ask questions to help you assess the points the speaker is making. *Keep an open mind.* Do not judge. Developing your listening skills benefits everyone.

Your Turn: Assess your listening behavior. What techniques can you use to improve your listening skills? Practice them the next time you have a conversation with someone.

Enrichment • Lesson 19

Type each line 2 times.

"
!
*
" ! *

A. NEW-KEY REINFORCEMENT

1 "If we go," Arif said, "we will need to find a substitute."
2 Goodness! I can't believe that! He must have been in shock!
3 The real reason* may never be known about those strangers.*
4 "Umberto's exact remarks* were shocking, to say the least!"

PPP   PRETEST » PRACTICE » POSTTEST

PRETEST
Take a 1-minute timed writing.

B. PRETEST: Discrimination Practice

5   Few of us were as lucky as Bev was when she joined us   12
6 for golf. She just dreaded the look of the work crew when   24
7 she goofed. But she neatly swung a club and aced the hole.   36
   1 | 2 | 3 | 4 | 5 | 6 | 7 | 8 | 9 | 10 | 11 | 12

PRACTICE
Speed Emphasis:
   If you made no more than 2 errors on the Pretest, type each *individual* line 2 times.
Accuracy Emphasis:
   If you made 3 or more errors, type each *group* of lines (as though it were a paragraph) 2 times.

C. PRACTICE: Left Hand

8 vbv behaves verb bevy vibes bevel brave above verbal bovine
9 wew dewdrop west weep threw wedge weave fewer weight sewing
10 ded precede deed seed bride guide dealt cried secede parted

D. PRACTICE: Right Hand

11 klk kindle kiln lake knoll lanky locks liken kettle knuckle
12 uyu untidy buys your usury unity youth buoys unruly younger
13 oio iodine coin lion oiled foils foist prior oilcan iodized

POSTTEST
Repeat the Pretest timed writing and compare performance.

E. POSTTEST: Discrimination Practice

Type each paragraph 2 times.

F. PARAGRAPH PRACTICE

14   Only a very few phlox grew or even bloomed just in   10
15 back of my old zinc quarry. I think the reason was that the 22
16 zinc had leached into the soil, making plants hard to grow. 34
17   She promptly judged the antique ivory buckles that   10
18 were made for the county fair. They won a prize. Next, we   22
19 moved on to judging the cakes and pies, which we all liked. 34
   1 | 2 | 3 | 4 | 5 | 6 | 7 | 8 | 9 | 10 | 11 | 12

Review

Goals

- Type at least 28wpm/2′/5e.

A. WARMUP

alphabet   1 West quickly gave Bert handsome prizes for six juicy plums.
number/symbol 2 gilp@comcast.net (11%) Ng & Ma 4/5 No! $13.86 *Est. #20-972
easy   3 Rodney may risk half of his profits for the old oak mantel.

Skillbuilding

B. NUMBER-KEY REVIEW

4 With 37,548 fans screaming, we won the game 10-9 on May 26.
5 He went to Rome on May 30, 1975, and left on July 24, 1986.
6 Seats 10, 29, 38, 47, and 56 are still unsold for tomorrow.
7 Our store will be open from 7:30 to 9:45 on February 18-26.

8 The 29 teachers and 754 students arrived at 8:30 on May 16.
9 Call 555-3190 and clarify our $826.47 charge for equipment.
10 Order No. 3874 for $165.20 did not arrive until October 19.
11 Al's sales for the last month went from $35,786 to $41,290.

C. PUNCTUATION REVIEW

.   12   Stand here. Sit down. Rest a minute. Relax. Breathe deeply.
?   13   Can it wait? Why not? Can he drive? Where is it? Who knows?
!   14   No! Stop! Don't look! Watch out! Move it over! Jump! Do it!
,   15   Inga, Lev, and I worked, rested, and then worked some more.

;   16   First, read the directions; next, practice; and then build.
:   17   Be on call at these times: 9:30, 12:30, 2:30, and 3:30 p.m.
-    18   It was a once-in-a-lifetime experience for Kay Jones-Lange.

'   19   It's Lynn's job to cover Maria's telephone when she's gone.
/   20   Two/thirds of us and one/fourth of them came on 12/10/2009.
"   21   I watched "Meet the Mets" and "Yankee Power" on the screen.

D. SYMBOL REVIEW

@   22   Order 12 items @ $114, 9 @ $99, and another 18 items @ $87.
#   23   My favorite seats for this year are #92, #83, #74, and #65.
$ 24   She received quotes of $48, $52, and $76 for the old radio.
%   25   Ramos scored 93% on the test, Sue had 88%, and Al made 84%.

&   26   Rudd & Sons bought their ten tickets from Cross & Thompson.
*   27   The * sign, the asterisk, is used for reference purposes.**
( )   28   The typist is (a) speedy, (b) accurate, and (c) productive.

E. MAP+: SYMBOLS

Follow the GDP software directions for this exercise to improve keystroking accuracy.

F. 12-SECOND SPEED SPRINTS

Take three 12-second timed writings on each line. The scale below the last line shows your wpm speed for a 12-second timed writing.

29   Kay and she may both visit us in May when they are in town.
30   She may go with me to the city to visit my son and his pal.
31   His body of work may charm the guests who visit the chapel.
32   That new city law may help us to fish for cod on the docks.
    ' ' ' '5' ' ' '10' ' ' '15' ' ' '20' ' ' '25' ' ' '30' ' ' '35' ' ' '40' ' ' '45' ' ' '50' ' ' '55' ' ' '60

G. 2-MINUTE TIMED WRITING

Take two 2-minute timed writings.

Goal: At least 28wpm/2'/5e

33   Jake or Peggy Zale must quickly fix the fax machine   11
34   so that we can have access to regional reports that we   22
35   think might be sent within the next few days. Without the   33
36   fax, we will not be able to finish all our monthly reports   45
37   by the deadline. Please let Peggy know of any problems.   56
    1 | 2 | 3 | 4 | 5 | 6 | 7 | 8 | 9 | 10 | 11 | 12

Enrichment • Lesson 20

Take a 1-minute timed writing on the boxed paragraph to establish your base speed. Then take a 1-minute timed writing on the following paragraph. As soon as you equal or exceed your base speed on this paragraph, move to the next, more difficult paragraph.

A. SUSTAINED PRACTICE: SYMBOLS

```
 1      It was quite normal that Patty was somewhat nervous as    11
 2  she entered the college building. After four years of work    23
 3  as a clerk, she was here to take the college entrance exam.    35

 4      Just as you have likely done, Patty took her #2 pencil    11
 5  and began to fill in the score sheet. A test administrator    23
 6  (Mr. Graham) had said that a grade of 75% would be passing.   35

 7      Patty had come to Room #68 (a large lecture hall) from    11
 8  the Stone & Carpenter accounting firm. It's a "mighty long    23
 9  hike," and almost 100% of the examinees were already there.   35

10      For a $25 fee, everyone in Room #68 (the test site)      11
11  answered the "moderately difficult" true-false or A/B/C/D     23
12  questions; 40% had used the Dun & Bradstreet study guide.     34
       1 | 2 | 3 | 4 | 5 | 6 | 7 | 8 | 9 | 10 | 11 | 12
```

Type each line 2 times. Type each sentence on a separate line by pressing ENTER after each sentence.

B. TECHNIQUE PRACTICE: ENTER KEY

```
13  Ed saw her. Ah. What? We do. Speak. Stop. Go. No. Begin it.
14  Thanks. Stop. Why not? See? Get it? Who, me? Well? She can.
15  See me. Who? Read it. What? Really! Why me? So soon? Do it.
16  Who knew? Enough? What is it? Go now. She did. Why not? So?
```

Type each line 2 times.

C. NUMBER PRACTICE

```
17  we 23 pro 049 too 599 wit 285 toe 593 wet 235 eye 363 IQ 81
18  pit 085 opts 9052 wow 292 quiz 1781 pep 030 pow 092 tow 592
19  you 697 tors 5942 ewe 323 tot 595 ere 343 wry 246 quit 1785
```

Type each paragraph 2 times.

D. PARAGRAPH TYPING

```
20      A campus TV quiz show just asked one contestant why     11
21  gold was buried at Fort Knox. No one knew the answer, so     22
22  they moved on to the business category, which was easier.    33

23      A few of the black taxis drove up the major road on     11
24  the hazy night. Because the hour was so late, they could     22
25  not find passengers needing rides, so they quickly left.     33

26      Jay took a big quiz and exam even though he suffered    11
27  a lower back pain that forced him to be very careful with    22
28  how he moved during the test. Fortunately, he aced it.      33
       1 | 2 | 3 | 4 | 5 | 6 | 7 | 8 | 9 | 10 | 11 | 12
```

Supplementary Lesson: Ten-Key Numeric Keypad

Goals

- Touch-type the ten-key numeric keypad keys.

New Keys

A. THE 4, 5, AND 6 KEYS

To input numbers using the ten-key numeric keypad, you must activate the NUM LOCK (Numeric Lock) key. Usually, an indicator light signals that the NUM LOCK is activated.

On the keypad, 4, 5, and 6 are the home-row keys. Place your fingers on the keypad home row as follows:

- J finger on 4
- K finger on 5
- L finger on 6

On most computers, there is a raised line or dot on the 5 key to help you easily locate the home-row position when using the keypad.

Use your Sem finger to control the ENTER key. For the exercises in A–F that follow:

1. Ensure that NUM LOCK is activated.
2. Press ENTER after typing the final digit of each number.
3. Type the first column from top to bottom; then move to the next column.
4. Keep your eyes on the copy.

1	444	455	466	544	566
2	555	644	656	456	654
3	666	445	466	554	556
4	664	665	456	654	454
5	464	546	564	655	456

B. THE 7, 8, AND 9 KEYS

Use the J finger to control the 7, the K finger to control the 8, and the L finger to control the 9.

6	474	585	696	549	984
7	747	858	969	485	645
8	774	885	996	658	489
9	447	558	669	846	647
10	744	855	966	476	867

C. THE 1, 2, AND 3 KEYS

Use the J finger to control the 1, the K finger to control the 2, and the L finger to control the 3.

11	414	525	636	215	326
12	141	225	336	634	435
13	144	552	663	324	145
14	441	255	636	263	346
15	144	252	363	431	265

D. THE 0 KEY

Use the right thumb to control the 0.

16	404	901	580	407	802
17	505	101	690	508	506
18	606	202	410	609	700
19	707	303	520	140	800
20	808	470	630	250	900

E. THE . KEY

Use the L finger to control the decimal (.) key.

21	6.6	7.6	1.2	6.5	9.8
22	3.2	4.4	7.7	5.5	8.8
23	2.2	6.6	9.3	1.1	1.0
24	3.1	8.4	7.1	9.3	3.4
25	4.5	8.3	9.9	6.5	3.8

Skillbuilding

F. NEW-KEY REVIEW

26	526	081	175	14.7	70.3	868	115
27	451	736	672	80.4	68.0	280	505
28	450	148	761	68.0	69.4	258	739
29	017	856	702	28.0	86.5	42	700
30	023	924	028	63.4	58.2	608	35
31	715	846	315	5.98	7.10	617	290
32	039	760	316	8.40	6.25	74	961
33	401	650	612	5.87	4.20	600	307
34	419	694	427	8.01	9.31	620	3
35	685	948	432	7.50	8.41	929	302

Enrichment • Supplementary Lesson

A. THE  KEY

Use the Sem finger to control the plus (+) key. Press the plus key after each number except the last number in a column. Press ENTER after the last number to display the total.

1	310+	698+	579+	747+	706+
2	845+	252+	999+	833+	126+
3	133+	320+	841+	599+	403+
4	603	484	782	738	180

B. THE KEY

Use the K finger to control the division (/) key. Press ENTER after the second number in each column to display the result.

5	858/728	912/771	814/238	542/236	956/895
6	595/104	527/970	739/129	771/292	590/485
7	121/494	181/376	984/533	814/820	836/237
8	696/998	293/432	160/189	485/181	922/172

C. THE KEY

Use the Sem finger to control the minus (-) key. Press ENTER after the second number in each column to display the result.

9	826-477	929-229	332-519	378-112	53.4-31.2
10	569-873	350-847	571-334	878-766	82.6-26.6
11	970-856	528-428	402-986	745-830	55.8-80.2
12	250-152	190-346	439-109	526-923	66.4-41.1

D. THE KEY

Use the L finger to control the multiplication (*) key. Press ENTER after the second number in each column to display the result.

13	406*363	733*835	923*419	645*618	21.8*18.6
14	214*331	554*843	492*103	135*889	58.8*70.7
15	199*927	572*604	756*375	276*942	84.4*77.1
16	885*286	778*358	601*793	192*672	19.3*99.0

E. NUMERIC KEYPAD REVIEW

Type the first column from top to bottom; then move to the next column. Press ENTER after the last number in each column to display the result.

17	933+	790/	338*	878-	512+	587+	764/
18	655-	835-	903+	444+	537*	25-	791-
19	175*	186*	579/	324/	890-	836*	762*
20	217	614	247	868	563	546	912

Skillbuilding

Skillbuilding

Progressive Practice: Alphabet

This skillbuilding routine contains a series of 30-second timed writings that range from 16 wpm to 104 wpm. The first time you use these timed writings, take a 1-minute timed writing with 3 or fewer errors on the Entry Timed Writing paragraph. Push moderately for speed.

Select a passage that is 1 to 2 wpm *higher* than your Entry Timed Writing speed. Then take up to six 30-second timed writings on the passage.

Your goal each time is to complete the passage within 30 seconds with no errors. When you have achieved your goal, move on to the next passage and repeat the procedure.

Entry Timed Writing

```
        Bev was very lucky when she found extra quality in the    11
home she was buying. She quietly told the builder that she         23
was extremely satisfied with the work done on her new home.        35
The builder said she can move into her new house next month.       47
       1  |  2  |  3  |  4  |  5  |  6  |  7  |  8  |  9  |  10  |  11  |  12
```

16 wpm

The author is the creator of a document.

18 wpm

Open means to access a previously saved file.

20 wpm

A byte represents one character to every computer.

22 wpm

Hard copy is usually text that is printed out on paper.

24 wpm

Soft copy is text that is displayed on your computer screen.

26 wpm

Memory is that part of your word processor that stores your data.

28 wpm

The menu is a list of choices used to guide a user through a function.

30 wpm

A sheet feeder is a device that will insert sheets of paper into a printer.

32 wpm

An icon is a small picture that illustrates a function or an object in software.

34 wpm

Active icons on your desktop represent the programs that can be run on your computer.

Skillbuilding

36 wpm	To execute means to perform an action specified by the user or also by a computer program.
38 wpm	Output is the result of a word processing operation. It can be either printed or magnetic form.
40 wpm	Format refers to the physical features which affect the appearance and arrangement of your document.
42 wpm	A font is a type style of a particular size or kind that includes letters, numbers, or punctuation marks.
44 wpm	Ergonomics is the science of adapting working conditions or equipment to meet the physical needs of employees.
46 wpm	Home position is the starting position of a document; it is typically the upper left corner of the display monitor.
48 wpm	The purpose of a virus checker is to find those programs that may cause your computer to stop working as you want it to.
50 wpm	An optical scanner is a device that can read text and enter it into a word processor without the need to type the data again.
52 wpm	Hardware refers to all the physical equipment you use while computing, such as the display screen, keyboard, printer, and scanner.
54 wpm	A peripheral device is any piece of equipment that will extend the capabilities of a computer system but is not required for operation.
56 wpm	A split screen displays two or more different images at the same time; it can, for example, display two different pages of a legal document.
58 wpm	To defrag the computer means that you are reorganizing the files so that related files will be located in the same general place on a hard drive.
60 wpm	With the click of a mouse, one can use a button bar or a toolbar for fast access to features that are frequently applied when using a Windows program.

Skillbuilding

62 wpm

Gadgets are typically controls which are placed on your desktop to allow you to have immediate access to frequently used information such as time and date.

64 wpm

Turnaround time is the length of time needed for a document to be keyboarded, edited, proofread, corrected if required, printed, and returned to the originator.

66 wpm

A local area network is a system that uses cable or another means to allow high-speed communication among many kinds of electronic equipment within particular areas.

68 wpm

To search and replace means to direct the word processor to locate a character, word, or group of words wherever it occurs in the document and replace it with newer text.

70 wpm

Indexing is the ability of a word processor to accumulate a list of words that appear in a document, including page numbers, and then print a revised list in alphabetic order.

72 wpm

When a program needs information from you, a dialog box will appear on the desktop. Once the dialog box appears, you must identify the option you desire and then choose the option.

74 wpm

A facsimile is an exact copy of a document, and it is also a process by which images, such as typed letters, graphs, and signatures, are scanned, transmitted, and then printed on paper.

76 wpm

Compatibility refers to when a computer is able to share information with other computers or also to communicate with different hardware. It could be accomplished by other methods.

78 wpm

Some operators like to personalize their desktops when they use Windows by making various changes. For example, they can change their screen colors or the pointer so that they will have more fun.

80 wpm

Wraparound is the ability of a word processor to move words from one line to another line and from one page to the next page as a result of inserting and deleting text or changing the size of margins.

82 wpm

It is possible when using Windows to evaluate the contents of different directories on the screen at the very same time. You can then choose to copy or move a particular file from one directory to another.

Skillbuilding

84 wpm

List processing is a capability of a word processor to keep lists of data that can be updated and sorted in alphabetic or numeric order. A list can also be added to any document that is stored in your computer.

86 wpm

A computer is a device that accepts data that are input and then processes those data to produce the output. A computer performs its work by using various stored programs that provide all the necessary instructions.

88 wpm

A word processor is more than a program that can process words. Word processors have many other capabilities such as merging documents; executing some mathematical equations; and inserting clip art, shapes, and pictures.

90 wpm

Help and support in Windows are available to assist you in finding answers to questions you may have about just how the computer functions. You can find help on topics like security, files, folders, printing, and maintenance.

92 wpm

When you want to look at the contents of two windows when using Windows, you might want to reduce the window size. Do this by pointing to a border or a corner of a window and dragging it until the window is the size that you want.

94 wpm

Scrolling means to display a very large quantity of text by rolling it horizontally or vertically past your display screen. As text disappears from the top section of your screen, new text will appear in the bottom area of your screen.

96 wpm

You have several options available to you when you print a document. For example, you can determine which printer to use, the pages you desire to print, the number of copies to be printed, the print quality desired, and the paper size used.

98 wpm

An ink-jet printer and a laser printer are popular printers used in a home office. Many users prefer an ink-jet printer because it is not as expensive to buy. But a laser printer provides a higher-quality print and is often the preferred choice.

Skillbuilding

100 wpm

E-mail, text messaging, cell phones, and chat rooms have enabled us to communicate quickly with people all around the globe. We can transmit a call or a message on the spur of the moment and receive a response to our call or message almost instantly.

102 wpm

Many different graphics software programs have been brought on the market in past years. These programs can be very powerful in helping with a business presentation. If there is a requirement to share data, using programs like these could be very helpful.

104 wpm

Voice mail is an essential service used by many people in the business world. This technology enables anyone placing a call to your phone to leave you a message if you cannot answer it at that time. This unique feature can help many workers be more productive.

Progressive Practice: Numbers

This skillbuilding routine contains a series of 30-second timed writings that range from 16 wpm to 80 wpm. The first time you use these timed writings, take a 1-minute timed writing with 3 or fewer errors on the Entry Timed Writing paragraph. Push moderately for speed.

Select a passage that is 1 to 2 wpm *higher* than your Entry Timed Writing speed. Then take up to six 30-second timed writings on the passage.

Your goal each time is to complete the passage within 30 seconds with no errors. When you have achieved your goal, move on to the next passage and repeat the procedure.

Entry Timed Writing

```
      Their bags were filled with 10 sets of jars, 23 cookie    11
cutters, 4 baking pans, 6 coffee mugs, 25 plates, 9 dessert    23
plates, 7 soup bowls, 125 recipe cards, and 8 recipe boxes.    35
David delivered these 217 items to 20487 Mountain Boulevard.   47
      1  |  2  |  3  |  4  |  5  |  6  |  7  |  8  |  9  |  10 | 11 | 12
```

16 wpm

There are 37 chairs in Rooms 24 and 156.

18 wpm

About 10 of the 39 boxes were torn on June 8.

20 wpm

Only 3 papers had errors on pages 28, 40, and 197.

22 wpm

My 46 letters were sent on May 10, June 3, and June 27.

24 wpm

The 79 freshmen, 86 juniors, and 54 seniors arrived at home.

26 wpm

The school needs 150 pens, 38 reams of paper, and 42 new folders.

28 wpm

Only 1 or 2 of the 305 new books had errors on pages 46, 178, and 192.

30 wpm

They met 10 of the 23 tennis players who received 4 awards from 5 trainers.

32 wpm

Those 8 vans carried 75 passengers on the first trip and 64 on the next 3 trips.

34 wpm

I saw 2 eagles on Route 86 and then 4 eagles on Route 53 at 9 a.m. on Monday, May 10.

Skillbuilding

36 wpm

The 17 firms produced 50 of the 62 records that received awards for 3 of the 4 categories.

38 wpm

The 12 trucks hauled 87 cows, 65 horses, and 49 pigs to the farm, which was 30 miles northeast.

40 wpm

She moved from 87 Bayview Drive to 659 Bay Street and then 3 blocks south to 4012 Gulbranson Avenue.

42 wpm

My 2 or 3 buyers ordered 5 dozen in sizes 6, 7, 8, and 9 after the 10 to 14 percent discounts were added.

44 wpm

There were 134 men and 121 women waiting in line at Gate 206 for the 58 to 79 tickets to the Cape Cod concert.

46 wpm

Steve had listed 5, 6, or 7 items on Purchase Order 243 when he saw that Purchase Requisition 89 contained 10 more.

48 wpm

Your items numbered 278 will sell for about 90 percent of the value of the 16 items that have code numbers shown as 435.

50 wpm

The managers stated that 98 of those 750 randomly selected new valves had about 264 defects, far exceeding the usual 31 norm.

52 wpm

Half of the 625 volunteers received over 90 percent of the charity pledges. Approximately 38 of the 147 agencies might enjoy this.

54 wpm

Merico hired 94 part-time workers to help the 378 full-time employees during the 62-day period when sales go up by 150 percent or more.

56 wpm

Kaye only hit 1 for 4 in the first 29 games after an 8-game streak in which she batted 3 for 4. She then hit at a .570 average for 16 games.

58 wpm

The mail carrier delivered 98 letters during the week to 734 Oak Street and also took 52 letters to 610 Faulkner Road as he returned on Route 58.

60 wpm

Pat said that about 1 in 5 of the 379 swimmers had a chance of being among the top 20. The best 6 of these 48 divers will receive special recognition.

Skillbuilding

62 wpm

It rained from 3 to 6 inches, and 18 of those 20 farmers were fearful that 4 to 7 inches more would flood about 95 acres along 3 miles of the new Route 79.

64 wpm

Those 17 sacks weighed 48 pounds, more than the 30 pounds that I had thought. All 24 believe the 92-pound bag is at least 15 or 16 pounds above its true weight.

66 wpm

They bought 7 of the 8 options for 54 of the 63 vehicles last month. They now have over 120 dump trucks for use in 9 of the 15 new regions in the big 20-county area.

68 wpm

Andy was 8 or 9 years old when they moved to 612 Glendale Street and away from the 700 block of Henry Lane, which is about 45 miles directly west of Boca Raton, FL 33434.

70 wpm

Doug had read 575 pages in the 760-page book by August 30; Darlene had read only 468 pages. Darlene has read 29 of those optional books since October 19, and Doug has read 18.

72 wpm

The school district has 985 elementary students, 507 middle school students, and 463 high school students. This total represents the greatest increase in total enrollment for us.

74 wpm

Attendance at last year's meeting was 10,835. Your goal for this year is to have 11,764 people. This might enable us to plan for an increase of 929 participants, a rise of 8.57 percent.

76 wpm

David's firm has 158 stores, located in 109 cities in the South. The company employs 3,540 males and 2,624 females, a total of 6,164 employees. About 4,750 of those employees work part-time.

78 wpm

Memberships were as follows: 98 members in the Drama Guild, 90 members in Zeta Tau, 82 members in Theta Phi, 75 in the Bowling Club, and 136 in the Ski Club. This meant that 481 joined the group.

80 wpm

The association had 684 members from the South, 830 members from the North, 1,023 members from the East, and 751 from the West. This total membership was 3,288; these numbers increased by 9.8 percent.

Paced Practice

The Paced Practice skillbuilding routine builds speed and accuracy in short, easy steps by using individualized goals and immediate feedback. You may use this program at any time after completing Lesson 9.

This section contains a series of 2-minute timed writings for speeds ranging from 16 wpm to 96 wpm. The first time you use these timed writings, take the 1-minute Entry Timed Writing with 2 or fewer uncorrected errors to establish your base speed.

Select a passage that is 2 wpm higher than your Entry Timed Writing speed. Then use this two-stage practice pattern to achieve each speed goal: (1) concentrate on speed and (2) work on accuracy.

Speed Goal. To determine your speed goal, take three 2-minute timed writings in total. Your goal each time is to complete the passage in 2 minutes without regard to errors. When you have achieved your speed goal, work on accuracy.

Accuracy Goal. To type accurately, you need to slow down—just a bit. Therefore, to reach your accuracy goal, drop back 2 wpm from the previous passage. Take consecutive timed writings on this passage until you can complete the passage in 2 minutes with no more than 2 errors.

For example, if you achieved a speed goal of 54 wpm, you should then work on an accuracy goal of 52 wpm. When you have achieved 52 wpm for accuracy, move up 4 wpm (for example, to the 56-wpm passage) and work for speed again.

Entry Timed Writing

If you can dream it, you can live it. Just follow your heart. There are many careers, which range from the mundane to the exotic to the sublime.

Start your career planning now by quizzing yourself about your talents, skills, and personal interests.

1 | 2 | 3 | 4 | 5 | 6 | 7 | 8 | 9 | 10 | 11 | 12

16 wpm

Your future is now, so you must seize every day.
After exploring your interests, quickly check the sixteen career clusters for a wide range of potential jobs.

18 wpm

When exploring various career options, think about what a job means for you.
Recognize that it can mean what you do just to earn money or what you find quite challenging overall.

20 wpm

If you acquire a job that you enjoy, then it means even more than simply earning an excellent wage.
It also means making a contribution, taking pride in your work, and utilizing all of your talents.

Skillbuilding

22 wpm

What is the difference between a job and a career? Think carefully. A job is work that you have to do for money.

A career is a sequence of related jobs that optimize your interests, experience, knowledge, and training.

24 wpm

Learn all about the world of work by looking at the sixteen career clusters. Most jobs are included in one of the clusters that have been organized by the government. When exploring careers, list all the unique clusters that interest you.

26 wpm

Once you identify the career clusters that interest you, look at the jobs that are within each cluster.

Analyze exactly what skills and aptitudes are needed, what training is required, what the work setting is like, and what your chances for advancement are.

28 wpm

Use your career center and your school or a public library to research your career choice. Go on the Internet, and ask experts for their unique views of certain careers.

As you gather data about your job options, you might learn about new career options that are on the horizon.

30 wpm

You must gain insight into a career. You can become a volunteer, sign up for an internship, or even work in a part-time job in the field.

You will become more familiar with a specific job while you develop your skills. You will quickly gain prized experience, whether you choose that career or not.

Skillbuilding

32 wpm

No matter which path you choose, strive for a high level of pride in yourself and in your job. Your image is affected by what other people think of you as well as by what you think of yourself.

Next, analyze your level of confidence. If you have any self-doubts, strive to acquire more self-confidence and self-esteem.

34 wpm

Confidence is required for a positive attitude, and a positive attitude is required for success at work. While you may not control all that happens at work, recognize that you must control how you react to what happens.

Become more confident and cultivate positive thoughts, which will provide you with extra power in life and on the job.

36 wpm

Quite a few factors lead to success on the job. People who have analyzed these factors say that it is the personal traits one exhibits that determine who is promoted and who is not.

One of the best traits a person can have is the trait of being likable. That means that you are honest, loyal, courteous, thoughtful, pleasant, kind, considerate, and positive.

38 wpm

If you are likable, you will relate well with most people. If you have excellent social contact with others, it will humanize the workplace and make your work there more enjoyable. Think of all the hours you are required to spend with one another each day.

If you show that you are willing to collaborate with your coworkers, most likely you will also receive their cooperation.

Skillbuilding

40 wpm

Cooperation begins on the first day of your new job. When you work for a firm, you quickly become a part of that team. Meeting people and learning new skills can be quite exciting.

For some people, though, a new situation can trigger some anxiety. The best advice is to remain calm, do your job with zeal, learn the workplace policies, be flexible, avoid being too critical, and always be positive.

42 wpm

When you begin a new job, even if you have recently received your college degree, chances are you will start at the bottom of the organizational chart. Each of us has to start somewhere. Do not despair or become lazy.

With hard work, you should start your climb up the corporate ladder. If you are smart, you will quietly take on even the most tedious task, take everything in stride, and exercise any chance to learn.

44 wpm

If you think learning is restricted to an academic setting, think again. You have much to learn on the job, even if it is a position for which you have been trained.

As a new employee, you will not be expected to know everything. When necessary, do not hesitate to ask your employer questions. Learn all you can about your job and the company. Capitalize on the new information to enhance your job performance and to build toward success.

46 wpm

Begin every valuable workday by prioritizing all of your tasks. Decide which tasks must be done immediately and which can wait. List the most important items first; then determine the order in which each item must be done.

After you complete a task, then quickly cross it off your priority list. Maximize your time; that is, do not put off work you should do. If a job must be done, just do it. You will stay on top of your list when you utilize time wisely.

Skillbuilding

48 wpm

Do not let the phone control your time. Learn how to
manage all your phone calls. Phone calls can be extremely
distracting from other duties, so be jealous of your quiet
time. When making a phone call, organize the topics you
want to discuss. Gather needed supplies such as pencils,
papers, and files.

Set a time limit and stick to the topic. Give concise
answers, summarize the points discussed, and end your talk
politely. Efficient phone usage will help you manage your
time.

50 wpm

As with everything, practice makes perfect, but along
the way, we have all made some mistakes. Realize that the
difference between successful people and those who are less
successful is not that the successful people make fewer
mistakes. It is just that they will never quit.

Instead of letting mistakes bring you down, use your
mistakes as opportunities to grow. If you make a mistake,
be patient with yourself. You might be able to fix your
mistake. Look for success to be just around the corner.

52 wpm

Be patient as you learn how to take care of problems
and accept criticism. Accepting criticism may be quite a
test for you. Still, it is vital to many of us at work.
Criticism that is given in a way to help you learn, expand,
or grow is called constructive criticism.

If you look at criticism as being helpful, it will be
easier to deal with. You might be amazed to learn that some
people welcome it since it teaches them the best way to
succeed on the job. Try to improve how you accept helpful
criticism from others.

Skillbuilding

54 wpm

People experience continuous growth during a career. Goal setting is a key tool to acquire for any job. Some people believe that goals provide the motivation we need to get to the place we want to be. Setting goals encourages greater achievements. The higher that we set our goals, the greater the effort we need to reach them.

Each time we reach a target or come closer to a goal, we should realize an increase in our confidence and in our performance, which leads to greater accomplishments. And the cycle continues to spiral for years.

56 wpm

One goal we must all strive for is punctuality. When employees are absent or just tardy, it costs the company money. If you are frequently tardy or absent, others have to do extra work to cover for you. If you are absent often, your peers may begin to resent you, which causes everyone stress in the department.

Being late and missing work might penalize your own relationship with your manager and have a negative effect on your career. To avoid such potential problems, develop a personal plan to ensure that you arrive every day on time and ready to work.

58 wpm

To hold a job is a chief part of being an adult. Some people start their work careers as teens. From the start, a range of work habits are developed that are as crucial to success as the actual job skills and knowledge that someone brings to his or her job.

What traits are expected of workers? What do employers look for when they rate their own workers? Vital personal traits would include being confident, helpful, positive, and loyal. If you are also kind, passionate, and organized, you may now have many of these qualities that employers value most of all in their staffs.

Skillbuilding

60 wpm

Being dependable is a required work trait. If a job
must be done by a special time, the manager will be pleased
to learn that his or her workers are going to meet that
deadline. Those who are dependable learn to utilize their
time to attain maximum results. Loyal workers can also be
counted on, they have good attendance records, they are
well prepared, and they get to work on time and ready to
start.

If the firm wants to meet its goals, it must have a
team of loyal and dependable workers. You, your peers, your
supervisors, and your managers are all team members who
work to reach their goals.

62 wpm

The ability to organize is an important quality for
the worker who would like to display good work habits. The
worker should have the ability to plan the work that needs
to be done and then to be able to execute that plan in a
timely manner.

An employer requires a competent worker to be well
organized. If the office worker is efficient, he or she
handles requests swiftly and deals with messages without
delay. The organized worker does not allow his or her work
to accumulate on the desk. Also, the organized worker will
return all phone calls quickly and make lists of the jobs
that still need to be done each day.

Skillbuilding

64 wpm

Efficiency is one work habit that is important. The efficient worker does each task quickly and starts work on the next task eagerly. He or she thinks about ways to save steps or time. For example, an efficient worker may plan just one trip to the copier with a number of copying jobs rather than take many trips to do each separate job.

Being efficient also means that you have all of the required supplies to finish each job. An efficient worker zips along on each project, uses his or her time wisely, and then stays focused on that one task. With careful and detailed planning, a worker who is efficient can finish tasks in less time.

66 wpm

Cooperation is another ideal work habit. It begins on the first day of the job and means that you quietly think of all team members when you make a decision. A person who cooperates is willing to do what is needed for the good of the whole group. For you to be a team player, you must take the extra steps to cooperate.

Cooperation may mean that you need to be a good sport if you are asked to do something you would rather not do. It may mean that you have to correct some mistakes made by another person in the office. When each employee has the interests of the company at heart and works well with other workers, then everyone is a good corporate citizen.

Skillbuilding

68 wpm

       Enthusiasm is still another work trait that is eagerly sought after by employers. If you are enthusiastic, then you have lots of positive energy. This is reflected in your actions toward your work, coworkers, and employer. It has been noted that eagerness can be catching. If you show you are excited to try any project, then you may quickly not only achieve the highest praise but also will be considered for career advancement.

       How much enthusiasm do you show at the workplace? Do you encourage people or complain to people? There should always be lots of good jobs for workers who are known to have a wealth of zeal and a positive approach to the jobs that they are assigned.

70 wpm

       Acceptance is a work trait required of all of us. In the work world of today, each business includes both men and women of different religions, races, cultures, skills, and beliefs. You will interact with many types of people as customers, coworkers, and owners. Treat each one fairly, openly, and honestly.

       All types of prejudice are hurtful, hateful, and, in short, unacceptable. Prejudice is not allowed at work. Each of us must learn to accept and even prize the many kinds of differences that are exhibited by all of us. Since so many diverse groups work side by side in the work world, it is vital that all workers maintain a high degree of shared insights. Embrace each of us for who we are.

Skillbuilding

72 wpm

It can be concluded that certain work habits or traits should play the major role in deciding the success of all workers. Most managers would be quick to agree on the high importance of these traits. It is most likely that these habits would be analyzed on performance appraisal forms. Promotions, pay increases, new duties, and your future with the company may be based on these yearly job assessments.

You should request regular job performance assessments even if your company does not conduct them. This feedback might then expand your job skills and career development by helping you grow. If you always look for ways to improve your work habits and skills, you will enjoy success in the world of work and beyond.

74 wpm

You can be sure that no matter where you work, you will use some form of technology. Almost every business depends on computers. Firms use such devices as voice mail, fax machines, cell phones, and personal digital assistants. These tools help us to do our work quickly and efficiently. They also take some of the drudgery out of our lives.

One result of the use of these tools is globalization, which means worldwide communication links between people. Our world has turned into one global village. We should expand our thinking beyond the office walls. We must become aware of what happens in other parts of the world. These events may directly affect you and your job. The more you know, the more valuable you will become to a company.

Skillbuilding

76 wpm

Each advance in technology has had an effect on all aspects of our lives. For example, the dawn of the age of the Internet has changed how people get and send data. It is the largest data network in the world. It is called the information superhighway since it is a vast network of big computers that can link people and resources around the world. It is an exciting medium to help you access current data and be more useful on the job and at home.

Without a doubt, we are all globally linked, and data technology services can support those links. The industry offers different job opportunities in dozens of fields. Keep in mind that keyboarding skills are required in this field as well as in most others. Touch-typing skills are just assumed in most jobs.

78 wpm

It is amazing to learn about the many jobs in which keyboarding skill is needed today. The use of a computer keyboard by executive chefs is a prime example. The chefs in large restaurants must prepare parts or all of the meals served while they direct the work of their staff of chefs, cooks, and others in and near the kitchens.

The computer has become a prime tool for a wide range of tasks, including tracking stocks of their food supplies. By seeing which items are favorites and which items are not requested, the chef can work out the food requirements, order food, and supervise the purchase of foods. Also, the computer has proved to be a very practical tool for such tasks as helping to plan budgets, prepare purchase orders for vendors, write menus, and print reports.

Skillbuilding

80 wpm

Advanced technology has opened the doors to a wide variety of amazing new products and services to sell. It seems that the more complex the products get, the higher the price of the products is and that the larger the sales commission is, the stiffer the competition is. To sell a technical product requires detailed product knowledge, good verbal skills, smooth sales rapport, and also expert typing skills.

Business favors those who have special training. For example, a pharmacy company may choose a person who has a strong knowledge of chemistry to sell its products. Sales is for those who enjoy using their command of persuasion to make the sales. The potential for good pay and commissions is quite high for the salesperson who is trained well. You should perhaps think about a job in sales.

82 wpm

As you travel about in your sales job or type a report at the office or create the Friday night pizza special for your new diner, you should always plan to put safety first. Accidents happen, but they do not have to happen regularly or to have such severe results. Accidents cost businesses billions of dollars each year in medical expenses, lost wages, and insurance claims.

Part of your job is to make certain that you are not one of the millions of people injured on the job each year. You may believe you work in a safe place, but accidents occur in all types of businesses. A few careless people cause most accidents, so ensure your safety on the job. Safety does not just happen. It is the result of the very careful awareness of those people who plan and put into action a safety program that benefits everyone.

Skillbuilding

84 wpm

In the world of today, you need more than the needed skills or the personal qualities to succeed on the job. Managers also expect all workers to have ethics. Ethics are the codes of conduct that tell a person or a group how to act. Workers who act ethically do not lie, cheat, or steal. They are honest and fair in all their dealings with others. In short, they are good citizens.

Workers who act ethically gain a good reputation for themselves and for their companies. They are known to be dependable. Unethical behavior can have a spiraling effect. A single act can do a lot of damage. Even if you have not held a job yet, you have had some experience with ethical problems. Life is full of a range of occasions to behave ethically. Do the right thing when faced with decisions. The ethics you follow will carry over into the workplace.

86 wpm

Now that you know what will be expected of you on the job, how do you make sure you will get the job in the first place? Almost everyone has at least once gone through the interview process for a job. For some, the interview is a traumatic event, but it does not have to be so stressful. Research is the key. Learn about the firm with whom you are seeking a job. Form a list of questions to ask. Interviews also provide you the chance to interview the organization.

Take a folder of items with you. Include copies of your data sheet with a list of three or more professional references, your academic transcript, and your certificates and licenses. Be sure to wear appropriate business attire. The outcome of the interview will be positive if you have enthusiasm for the job, match your skills to the needs of the company, ask relevant questions, and listen.

Skillbuilding

88 wpm

How can you be the strongest candidate for the job? Be sure that your skills in reading, writing, math, speaking, and listening are strong. These skills should enable you to listen well and communicate clearly, not only during the job interview but also at your place of work. This exchange of information between a sender and a receiver is known as communication.

It does not matter which career you choose; you will still spend most of your time using these basic skills to communicate with others. You should use the skills as tools to gain information, solve problems, and share ideas. You can also use these skills to help you meet the needs of your customers. Most of the new jobs in the next few years will be in industries that will require direct customer contact. Do not jeopardize your chances for success; make sure that you are able to communicate well with others.

90 wpm

Writing well can help you gain a competitive edge in your job search and throughout your career. Most of us have had occasion to write business letters whether to apply for a job, to comment on a product or service, or to place an order. Often it seems easy to sit back and let our thoughts flow freely. At other times, we seem to struggle to find the best words to use to express our thoughts in precisely the correct way. We all sometimes have these issues.

Writing skills can improve with practice. Use these principles to develop your writing skills. Try to use words that you would be comfortable using in person. Use words that are simple, direct, kind, and confident. When it is possible, use words that emphasize only the positive side. Remember to proofread your work. Well-organized thoughts and proper grammar, spelling, and punctuation will show your reader that you care about quality.

Skillbuilding

Skillbuilding

92 wpm

Listening is such a vital part of the communication process. It is the key for learning, getting along, and forming rapport. Do you think that you are an active or a passive listener? Listening should not be just a passive process. To listen actively means to analyze what is being said and to interpret what it means. Active listening makes you a more effective worker because you react to what you have heard as well as to what you have not heard.

Study these steps to expand your listening skills: Do not cut people off; let them finish their remarks before you speak. If what they said is unclear, write down your questions, and wait for the discussion to be finished until you ask them. Reduce personal and environmental noise so you can focus on the message. Keep an open mind. Remain attentive and maintain eye contact when possible. By using these skills, you can become even more confident and more effective.

94 wpm

Speaking is also a form of communication. In the world of work, speaking is an important way in which to share information. Regardless of whether you are speaking to an audience of one or one hundred, you will want to be sure that your listeners hear your message. Be clear about your purpose, your audience, and your subject. A purpose is the overall goal or reason for speaking. An audience is anyone who receives information. The subject is the main topic or key idea that you wish to analyze.

Research your subject. Use specific facts and examples to give you credibility. As you speak, be brief and direct. Progress logically from point to point. Speak slowly and pronounce clearly all your words. Is the quality of your voice friendly and pleasant or is it shrill and offensive? These factors influence how your message is received. A good idea is worthless if you cannot present it well, so take all the time you need to get ready.

Skillbuilding

96 wpm

Building a career is a process. You have looked at all your interests, values, skills, talents, and feelings. Your look into the world of work has begun, but the journey does not stop here, for the present is the perfect place to start thinking about the future. It is where you start to take steps toward your goals. It is where you can really make a difference.

As you set personal and career goals, remember the importance of small steps. Each step toward a personal goal or a career goal is a small victory. The feeling of success encourages you to take other small steps. Each step builds onto the next. Continue analyzing your personal world as well as the world you share with others. Expect the best as you go forward. Expect a happy life, loving relationships, success in life, and fulfilling and satisfying work in a job that you really love. Last but not least, expect that you have something unique and special to offer the world, because you do.

Skillbuilding

Supplementary Timed Writings

All problem solving, whether or not it is personal or 11
academic, involves decision making. You make decisions in 23
order to solve problems. On occasion, a problem occurs as a 35
result of a decision you have made. For example, you may 46
decide to smoke, but later in life, you might then face the 58
problem of nicotine addiction. You may decide not to study 70
math and science because you think that they are difficult. 82

Because of this choice, some career options may be 93
closed to you. There is a consequence for each action. Do 108
you see that events in your life do not just happen, but 116
that they are the result of your choices and decisions? 127

How can you best prepare your mind to help you solve 138
problems? A positive attitude is a great start. Indeed, 149
your attitude will determine the way in which you may solve 161
a problem or make a decision. Approach your studies, such 173
as science and math courses, with a positive attitude. Try 185
to think of academic problems as puzzles to be solved and 195
not just as work to be avoided. 203

Critical thinking is a type of problem solving that 213
allows you to decode, analyze, reason, assess, and process 224
data. Since it is basic for all successful problem solving, 235
you should try to explore, probe, question, and search for 248
all the right answers. 253

A problem may not always be solved on the first try, 263
so do not give up. Try, try again. To find a solution may 275
take a real effort. Use your critical thinking skills to 286
achieve success in a world that is highly competitive and 298
demanding. 300

1 | 2 | 3 | 4 | 5 | 6 | 7 | 8 | 9 | 10 | 11 | 12

Skillbuilding

For many of us, the Internet is an important resource   11
in our private and public lives. The Internet provides us   23
with quick access to countless Web sites that may contain   34
news, products, games, and other types of data. The Web   45
pages on these sites can be designed, authored, and posted   57
by anyone from anywhere around the world, so you must use   69
critical thinking skills when reviewing these Web sites.   80

Just because something is said on the radio, printed   91
in the newspaper, or shown on television does not mean that   103
it is true. This applies to data found on the Internet as   115
well. Do not fall into the trap of believing that if it is   126
on the Net, it must be true. A wise user of the Internet   138
thinks critically about data found on the Net and evaluates   150
this material before he or she decides to use it.   160

When you assess a new Web site, think about who, what,   171
how, when, and where. Who refers to the author of the Web   183
site. The author may be a business firm, an organization,   194
or a person. What refers to the validity of the data. Can   206
this data be verified by a reputable source?   215

How refers to the viewpoint of the author. Are your   225
data presented without prejudice? When refers to the time   237
frame of your data. Do you have recent data? Where refers   249
to your data source. Are the data from a trusted source?   260

By answering these critical questions, you will learn   271
more about the accuracy and dependability of a Web site.   283
When you surf the Net next time, be quite cautious. Anyone   294
can publish on the Internet.   300

1 | 2 | 3 | 4 | 5 | 6 | 7 | 8 | 9 | 10 | 11 | 12

Skillbuilding

Most office workers perform a wide range of tasks in   11
their workday. These tasks may require them to handle phone   23
calls or forward personal messages, to send short e-mail   34
notes or compile complex office reports, or to write simple   46
letters or assemble detailed letters with tables, graphics,   58
and imported data. Office workers are thus a basic part of   70
the structure of the firm.   75

The office worker must use critical thinking in order   86
to carry out a wide array of daily tasks. Some of the tasks   98
are more urgent than other tasks and should be done first.   110
Some tasks take only a short time, while others take a lot   122
more time. Some tasks demand a quick response, while others   134
may be taken up as time permits or even postponed until the   146
future. Some of these tasks might require input from other   158
people.   159

Whether a job is simple or complex or big or small,   170
the office worker must decide what is to be done first by   182
setting the priority for each task.   189

When setting priorities, critical thinking skills are   200
essential. The office worker must assess each aspect of the   212
task. It is a good idea to identify the size of the task,   223
learn about its complexity, estimate the effort needed,   235
judge its importance, and set its deadline.   243

Once the office worker assesses a task that is to be   254
done within a certain span of time, then the priority for   266
completing all those tasks can be set. Critical thinking   277
skills, if applied well, can save the employer money, but   289
if they are applied poorly, they might cost an employer.   300

1 | 2 | 3 | 4 | 5 | 6 | 7 | 8 | 9 | 10 | 11 | 12

Skillbuilding

Skillbuilding

Supplementary Timed Writing 4

Each day business managers must make choices that keep 11
their firms running in a smooth, skillful, and gainful way. 23
Every decision needs to be quick and sure. 32

To make good decisions, all managers must use critical 43
thinking. They must gather all the needed facts so that 54
they can make sound, well-informed choices. Over time, they 66
can refine their skills. Then, when they face a similar 77
problem, they can use their knowledge to help them solve 89
new problems with ease and in less time. 97

What types of decisions do you think managers make 107
that involve critical thinking? Human resource managers 119
need to decide whom to hire, what to pay the new worker, 130
and where to place him or her. In addition, human resource 142
managers should be able to help resolve conflicts between 153
workers. 155

Office managers must purchase copy machines, software, 166
computers, and supplies. Top executives must make business 178
policies, appoint other managers, and assess the success of 190
the firm. Plant supervisors must set schedules, gauge work 202
quality, and assess workers. Sales managers must study all 214
of the new sales trends, as well as provide sales training. 226

Most managers use critical thinking to make wise and 237
well-thought-out decisions. They carefully check all the 248
facts, analyze these facts, and then make a final judgment 259
based upon these facts. They should also be able to clearly 271
discern fact from fiction. Through trial and error, most 283
managers learn their own ways to solve problems and find a 294
solution for their firms. 300

1 | 2 | 3 | 4 | 5 | 6 | 7 | 8 | 9 | 10 | 11 | 12

Skillbuilding

Supplementary Timed Writing 5

In most classes, teachers just want the students to 11
analyze situations, draw conclusions, and solve problems. 22
Each of these tasks requires students to use good thinking 34
skills. How do students acquire these skills? What process 46
do students follow to develop these skills? 55

During early years of life, children learn words and 65
then combine these words into sentences. From there, they 77
learn to declare ideas, share thoughts, and express their 89
feelings. Students learn numbers and math concepts. They 100
may learn to read musical notes, to keep rhythm, to sing 111
songs, and to recognize popular and classical pieces of 123
music. Students learn colors and shapes and start to draw. 134

During their early years, students learn the basic 145
models of problem solving. One way for students to solve 156
problems and apply thinking skills is to use the scientific 168
approach. This approach requires a student to state the 179
problem to be solved, collect the known facts about that 191
problem, analyze the problem, and pose viable solutions. 202
Throughout this process, teachers ask questions that force 214
students to expand their thinking skills. 222

Teachers may want to ask questions such as these: Did 233
you clearly state the problem? Did you get all the facts? 245
Did you get the facts from the right place? Did you assume 257
anything? Did you pose other possible answers? Did you keep 269
an open mind to all solutions? Did you let your bias come 280
into play? Did you take the time to listen to other people? 292
Finally, does the solution make sense? 300

1 | 2 | 3 | 4 | 5 | 6 | 7 | 8 | 9 | 10 | 11 | 12

Skillbuilding

A major goal for all instructors in school is to teach 11
critical thinking skills to their class. This skill is the 23
process of deciding in a logical way what we should do or 35
believe, and it also involves an ability to compare and 46
contrast, solve problems, make decisions, analyze results, 58
and combine and use knowledge. Can you see that these are 69
important skills you can use all your life? 78

These skills help the student who later becomes a part 89
of the workforce. Whether someone is in a small business, 101
is in a corporate setting, or is self-employed, the world 112
of today is a competitive one, and skilled employees are 124
always in demand. 127

One part of gaining success in the workforce is having 139
the skill to deal with the mixed demands of the fast-paced 150
business world. A few of the required skills are insightful 162
decision making, creative problem solving, and productive 174
contact among diverse groups. 180

In school, we learn the basics of critical thinking. 191
This skill extends far beyond the borders of the classroom 203
and lasts a lifetime. We use critical thinking in all of 214
our daily lives. We constantly analyze and assess pursuits 226
such as music, movies, speech, fashion, magazine articles, 238
and television shows. 242

We all had experience using critical thinking skills 253
well before we even knew what they were. So you should keep 265
on learning and growing. The classroom can be the perfect 276
place for your exploration, so use that time to learn how 288
others solve problems. There are always new goals to reach. 300

1 | 2 | 3 | 4 | 5 | 6 | 7 | 8 | 9 | 10 | 11 | 12

Skillbuilding

Supplementary Timed Writing 7

One of the first steps you should take to unlock your 11
creativity is to realize that you have control over your 22
mind; your mind does not control you. Creativity is just 34
using a new or different way to solve a problem. 44

Many of our inventions have involved breakthroughs in 55
traditional ways of thinking, and the result has often been 67
amazing. For example, Einstein broke with the old ways and 78
tried obscure formulas that have changed all scientific 90
thought. Your attitude can form a mental block that may 101
keep you from exercising creativity. When you free up your 113
mind, the rest will follow. 118

Do your best to unleash your mind's innate creativity 129
by turning problems into puzzles. When you think of the 140
task as a puzzle, a challenge, or a game instead of as a 152
difficult problem, you will open up your mind and free your 164
creative side to operate. Creative ideas come when you are 176
enjoying yourself and are involved in unrelated tasks. 187

Old habits often restrict you from trying new ways of 198
solving problems. There is often more than one solution, so 210
strive to see each situation in a fresh, new light. How 221
many times have you told yourself that you must follow the 233
rules and perform tasks only in a certain way? 242

If you want to be creative, then look at situations in 253
a new light, break the pattern, explore new opportunities, 265
and challenge old rules. If you are facing a hard problem 277
and cannot find an answer, take a quick walk or relax for a 289
few minutes; you can then go back to the problem renewed. 300

1 | 2 | 3 | 4 | 5 | 6 | 7 | 8 | 9 | 10 | 11 | 12

Skillbuilding

Supplementary Timed Writing 8

Keyboarding is a very popular business course that 10
most students take. The major goals of a keyboarding course 22
are to develop touch control of the keyboard, to use proper 34
typing techniques, to build basic speed and accuracy, and 46
to receive considerable practice in applying those basic 57
skills to format letters, reports, tables, memos, and other 69
kinds of personal and business documents. 78

In the first part of a keyboarding course, you must 88
learn to stroke the keys by touch, using proven techniques. 100
You learn to strike the keys in a quick and accurate way. 112
After the keys are learned, you then focus your attention 123
on producing documents of many sizes and types. 133

When you first learn to keyboard, there may be certain 144
steps, guidelines, and exercises that should be followed. 156
There are rules to help you learn and in due time to master 168
the keyboard. To create each document requires that you 179
apply critical thinking. What format or layout should be 190
used? What font and font size would be best? Are all the 202
words spelled correctly? Does the document look neat on the 214
page? Are the figures accurate? Are the punctuation and 225
grammar correct? 228

Being creative also has a lot to do with risk taking 239
and courage. It takes courage to explore new ways to think 251
and to risk looking different and even to risk being wrong. 263
Your path to creativity is such a vital component of your 274
critical thinking skills. Allow your creative thoughts to 286
flow freely when you produce each keyboarding task. Enjoy 298
the journey. 300

1 | 2 | 3 | 4 | 5 | 6 | 7 | 8 | 9 | 10 | 11 | 12

Skillbuilding

More employees are injured using the computer keyboard 11
in the United States than using any other equipment in the 23
workplace. Therefore, you should find the most comfortable 35
and ergonomic position when you are keyboarding. 45

Your chair should be on rollers, be adjustable to fit 56
your individual height, and have substantial support for 67
your lower back. You should sit with your hips pushed as 78
far back in the chair as possible, and your thighs should 90
not touch the underside of the workstation. 99

Your monitor should be aligned with your keyboard and 110
centered opposite you. The display should be just slightly 122
below eye level and tilted away from you slightly. When you 134
sit back in the chair and hold your arm out horizontally, 145
your middle finger should touch the middle of the monitor. 157
That way you won't need to make excessive head movements to 169
see the viewing area of your screen. 176

A document holder should be positioned at the same 187
height and distance as the screen in order to minimize any 199
head movements and at the same angle as the screen. Place 210
the document holder to the side of the screen opposite the 222
mouse. Position the mouse at the identical height as the 233
keyboard, and you should move the mouse with your whole arm 245
and not just with your wrist. 251

There's no research to show that an ergonomic keyboard 263
is any more beneficial than the standard keyboard layout. 274
If your keyboard has pop-up legs, these should not be used 286
because a negative slope to the keyboard is by far the most 298
healthful. 300

1 | 2 | 3 | 4 | 5 | 6 | 7 | 8 | 9 | 10 | 11 | 12

Skillbuilding

One of the most important decisions we all have to 10
face is choosing a career. Your options can appear to be a 22
bit overwhelming at first. But you should not worry because 34
your critical thinking skills will help. 42

Start with a self-assessment. What are your interests? 54
Would you prefer to work inside or outdoors? Would you like 66
to work with numbers or with words? Are you an independent 77
type or would you rather work within a group? What are your 89
preferred courses? Think about each of these questions, and 101
then make a list of your interests, skills, aptitudes, and 113
values. What you learn about yourself might help you find 125
the career that is just right for you. 133

After you have explored your own interests, look at 143
the sixteen career clusters for a wide range of possible 155
jobs. Most jobs are included in one of these clusters that 166
have been organized by the government. During your search, 178
make a note of the clusters that interest you and look into 190
all the clusters. 194

Get as much information as you can by making use of 204
all available resources. Scan the employment section in the 216
major Sunday newspapers for job descriptions and salaries. 228
Search the Internet, which provides access to job listings 240
around the world. If you want to evaluate closely a certain 252
company, access its home page and look around. 261

Sign up for interviews with companies that visit your 272
campus. Talk with people in your field of interest to ask 284
questions and get advice. Taking the initiative in your job 296
search will pay off. 300

1 | 2 | 3 | 4 | 5 | 6 | 7 | 8 | 9 | 10 | 11 | 12

Index

NOTE: Page numbers preceded by R- indicate material in References Manual; page numbers preceded by SB- indicate material in Skillbuilding supplement.